Leader Book

Acts: model for today's church

Bible Study That Builds Christian Community

SERENDIPITY HOUSE

LIFE CONNECTIONS

ISBN: 1-5749-4098-8

To order additional copies of this resource:
ORDER ONLINE at *www.serendipityhouse.com*;
VISIT the LifeWay Christian Store serving you;
WRITE Serendipity House
117 10th Avenue, North
Nashville, TN 37234
FAX (615) 277-8181
PHONE (800) 525-9563

Printed in the United States of America

SERENDIPITY HOUSE
117 10th Avenue, North
Nashville, Tennessee 37234

Contents

Core Values

Community: The purpose of this curriculum is to build community within the body of believers around Jesus Christ.

Group Process: To build community, the curriculum must be designed to take a group through a step-by-step process of sharing your story with one another.

Interactive Bible Study: To share your "story," the approach to Scripture in the curriculum needs to be open-ended and right-brained—to "level the playing field" and encourage everyone to share.

Developmental Stages: To provide a healthy program in the life cycle of a group, the curriculum needs to offer courses on three levels of commitment:

(1) **Beginner Level**—low-level entry, high structure, to level the playing field;
(2) **Growth Level**—deeper Bible study, flexible structure, to encourage group accountability;
(3) **Discipleship Level**—in-depth Bible study, open structure, to move the group into high gear.

Target Audiences: To build community throughout the culture of the church, the curriculum needs to be flexible, adaptable, and transferable into the structure of the average church.

Mission: To expand the kingdom of God one person at a time by filling the "empty chair." (We add an extra chair to each group session to remind us of our mission.)

Group Covenant

It is important that your group covenant together, agreeing to live out important group values. Once these values are agreed upon, your group will be on its way to experiencing Christian community. It's very important that your group discuss these values—preferably as you begin this study. The first session would be most appropriate. (Check the rules to which each member of your group agrees.)

- ▢ **Priority:** While you are in this course of study, you give the group meetings priority.
- ▢ **Participation:** Everyone is encouraged to participate and no one dominates.
- ▢ **Respect:** Everyone is given the right to his or her own opinion, and all questions are encouraged and respected.
- ▢ **Confidentiality:** Anything that is said in the meeting is never repeated outside the meeting.
- ▢ **Life Change:** We will regularly assess our own life-change goals and encourage one another in our pursuit of Christlikeness.
- ▢ **Empty Chair:** The group stays open to reaching new people at every meeting.
- ▢ **Care and Support:** Permission is given to call upon each other at any time, especially in times of crisis. The group will provide care for every member.
- ▢ **Accountability:** We agree to let the members of the group hold us accountable to the commitments we make in whatever loving ways we decide upon.
- ▢ **Mission:** We will do everything in our power to start a new group.
- ▢ **Ministry:** The group will encourage one another to volunteer and serve in a ministry and to support missions by giving financially and/or personally serving.

For the Leader

Each group meeting consists of a three-part agenda:

Icebreaker – Fun questions designed to warm the group and build understanding about other group members. These questions prepare the group for meaningful discussion throughout the session.

Bible Study – The heart of each session is the Bible study time. The Life Connections series involves six easy-to-understand segments.

1. **Scripture Reading** – Each Bible study begins with the reading of the focal passage.
2. **About Today's Session** – This section of the Bible Study time is designed to peak the interest of attendees and introduce the theme for the session. In most instances there will be a reminder of what was studied the previous week, a captivating illustration or analogy related to everyday life, and a statement describing what life-changing topic will be given attention.
3. **Identifying with the Story** – During this segment of the Bible Study, subgroups learn more about each other by answering questions that will help them share their story. These questions directly relate to the topic for the day.
4. **Today's Session** – This short teaching time will be led by the Master Teacher. These scripted teachings include a depth of biblical understanding, fascinating illustrations, analogies, statistics, and stories that will spark questions and conviction.
5. **Learning from the Story** – Subgroups will gather to answer a series of questions that anticipate commitment to applying the truths taught.
6. **Life Change Lessons** – The Master Teacher gives practical suggestions that will aid attendees in carrying out the commitments they make.

Caring Time – All study should point us to action. Each session ends with prayer and direction in caring for the needs of group members. Time is also provided to pray for the "empty chair." The empty chair is a visible symbol of the need for each group to lead an unbeliever to a relationship with Jesus Christ.

The cross icon and boxed text represents portions of the student book that have been reprinted in this book.

Every Life Connections group must fill three important roles. Each responsibility is vital to the success of the class.

Teacher – The teacher is the key leader of any Life Connections group. It is the responsibility of the teacher to:

1. enlist facilitators and apprentices.
2. make facilitators and apprentices aware of their roles and be certain these responsibilities are carried out.
3. meet periodically with facilitators to train, encourage, and inspire them.
4. cast vision for and keep the group focused on the goals of the group.
5. guide group members to understand and commit to the group covenant.
6. be sure the group utilizes, fills, and evangelizes through use of the empty chair concept.
7. act as the Master Teacher for the group.
8. keep the group on task throughout each session.

Facilitator – Each subgroup will have a facilitator.
It is the responsibility of the facilitators to:

1. lead each individual in their subgroup to participate in Icebreaker activities.
2. involve all members in their subgroup in the Identifying with the Story section of the study.
3. guide those in their subgroup to commit to apply the lessons learned in the Learning from the Story section of the weekly session.
4. with sensitivity and wisdom lead their subgroup to minister to one another during the Caring Time and involve their subgroup in ministry and evangelism.
5. minister to the needs of their subgroup members and lead them to minister to the needs of one another both during and between meetings.

Apprentice – Every subgroup must have an apprentice. When the group consistently has eight or more in attendance, the group should divide into two groups. The apprentice will become the facilitator of the new group and choose an apprentice who will someday be the facilitator of a group. It is the role of the apprentice to:

1. learn from the facilitator of their group.
2. make welcome all new subgroup members.
3. be certain student books and pens or pencils are available for all participants.
4. turn in prayer requests.
5. encourage participation by actively participating themselves.
6. lead the group when the facilitator is unavailable.

For more information and frequently asked questions about Life Connections, visit our Web site at *www.serendipityhouse.com*.

Session

1

Called to Action

Prepare for the Session

	READINGS	REFLECTIVE QUESTIONS
Monday	Acts 1:1–3	What has Christ done to show you that He is alive?
Tuesday	Acts 1:4–8	Where is Christ calling you to witness this week?
Wednesday	Acts 1:9	What "cloud" sometimes hides Christ from you? How can you dispel this "cloud"?
Thursday	Acts 1:10–11	What are you doing to make sure you are prepared when Christ returns?
Friday	Acts 1:14	How well are you disciplining yourself in prayer? Is your prayer life "hit-and-miss" or are you going to God regularly?
Saturday	Acts 1:15–17	When has one you considered a Christian friend failed you? How well are you dealing with that failure?
Sunday	Acts 1:24	What is God, who knows your heart, calling you to do with your life right now?

notes:

OUR GOALS FOR THIS SESSION ARE:

In groups of 6–8, gather people in a horseshoe configuration.

Make sure everyone has a name tag.

Take time to share information on class parties that are coming up as well as any relevant church events.

INTRODUCE THE ICEBREAKER ACTIVITY: The students have been told in their books to choose one answer.

After the Icebreaker say something like, "We have all had our difficult good-byes. One of the hardest good-byes in history was when Jesus ascended into heaven and left His disciples to manage without His earthly presence. We will look at what that experience meant to them in today's session."

Hand out the Prayer/Praise Report. A sample copy is on pages 158-159. Have people write down prayer requests and praises. Then have the prayer coordinator collect the report and make copies for use during the Caring Time.

BIBLE STUDY
- to consider Jesus' last words to His disciples and how His words apply to our mission
- to better understand what we are called to do in relationship to what God is doing in the world
- to begin looking at the role of the Holy Spirit in empowering the church to action

1

LIFE CHANGE
- to adopt a missionary
- to visit a local ministry in our hometown
- to spend some time in conversation with a non-Christian acquaintance or loved one

Icebreaker (10-15 minutes)

Saying Good-byes. Go around the group on question 1 and let everyone share. Then go around again on question 2.

1. In which of the following life situations did you have the hardest time saying good-bye? Mark your answer with an "H." In which of these situations did you have the easiest time? Mark your answer with an "E."

___ when I first went to kindergarten
___ when I got married or left home to go to college
___ when I graduated from high school and had to say good-bye to friends
___ when I left my first job
___ when a pastor at my church left for another position
___ when my first child went to kindergarten
___ when my child got married or left home to go to college

2. When it comes to saying good-bye, which of the following approaches do you most often use?

☐ I drag out all the hugs and tears for as long as I can.
☐ I make it quick and painless.
☐ I just leave and don't say anything.

notes:

LEARNING FROM THE BIBLE

ACTS 1:1-11

Have four members of the class, selected ahead of time, read the Scripture for today from Acts. Ask one person to read the narrative portion, another to read the part of Jesus (vv. 7-8), and the other two the part of the angels (v. 11). The whole class should read the words of the disciples in verse 6.

Bible Study (30-45 minutes)

The Scripture for this week:

*[1]In my former book, Theophilus, I wrote about all that Jesus
began to do and to teach [2]until the day he was taken up to heaven,
after giving instructions through the Holy Spirit to the apostles he
had chosen. [3]After his suffering, he showed himself to these men and
gave many convincing proofs that he was alive. He appeared to them
over a period of forty days and spoke about the kingdom of God. [4]On
one occasion, while he was eating with them, he gave them this
command: "Do not leave Jerusalem, but wait for the gift my Father
promised, which you have heard me speak about. [5]For John baptized
with water, but in a few days you will be baptized with the Holy Spirit."*

*[6]So when they met together, they asked him, "Lord, are you at
this time going to restore the kingdom to Israel?"*

*[7]He said to them: "It is not for you to know the times or dates the
Father has set by his own authority. [8]But you will receive power when
the Holy Spirit comes on you; and you will be my witnesses in Jerusalem,
and in all Judea and Samaria, and to the ends of the earth."*

*[9]After he said this, he was taken up before their very eyes, and a
cloud hid him from their sight.*

*[10]They were looking intently up into the sky as he was going,
when suddenly two men dressed in white stood beside them. [11]"Men
of Galilee," they said, "why do you stand here looking into the sky?
This same Jesus, who has been taken from you into heaven, will come
back in the same way you have seen him go into heaven."*

notes:

Summarize these introductory remarks. Be sure to include the underlined information, which gives the answers to the student book questions (provided in the margin).

What are people who fail to learn from church history doomed to do?

What should a church do when the members feel they are not doing any kind of mighty work for the Lord?

...about today's session (5 minutes)

THE CHURCH'S POWER SOURCE

An oft-quoted saying is, "Those who fail to learn from history are doomed to repeat it." That saying might work well when you are talking about the history of wars and catastrophes, but when you're talking about the history of the early church, as recorded in Acts, it would be more appropriate to say, "Those who fail to learn from history are doomed *not* to repeat it." The history of the church in Acts includes many mighty works that were done through the guidance and power of the Holy Spirit. Whenever church members of today feel like they are not doing any kind of mighty work for the Lord, they need to look back at the stories of Acts and remember that the Holy Spirit is their source of power.

Getting back in touch with the church's power source is exactly what we will be doing in this course on the Book of Acts. In today's session in particular, we will look at what happened when Jesus first left the disciples to carry on His work. While He had assured them that He was with them always (Matt. 28:20), and promised that the Holy Spirit would give them power (Acts 1:8), they would still be "on their own" in the sense of making earthly decisions about Christ's work. In this new life situation, would they fully utilize the power made available to them? Do we fully utilize the Holy Spirit's power in our daily lives? That is what we will be considering today.

notes:

Remain in groups of 6–8 people, in a horseshoe configuration.

In this small-group session, students will be responding to the following questions that will help them share their stories in terms of the ascension of Christ in Acts 1:1-11.

Have the students explore these questions together.

Identifying with the Story (5-7 minutes)

1. When you were an adolescent or younger adult, who did you consider to be your mentor? In what area of life did you learn the most from this person?

2. How would you describe your mentoring status right now in terms of this story?
   - ☐ I'm still receiving mentoring, like the apostles did during the 40 days.
   - ☐ I'm desiring mentoring, like the apostles did after Jesus ascended.
   - ☐ I'm ready to act on my own, like the disciples did later at Pentecost.
   - ☐ I'm ready to mentor others, like Luke did through the writing of Acts.
   - ☐ I'm not sure that I would be comfortable either mentoring or being mentored.

3. Had you been with Jesus when He was getting ready to return to heaven, what one last question would you have asked Him?

notes:

today's session (15-20 minutes)

Share with your class the following information which you may modify according to your own perspectives and teaching needs. The answers to the student book questions (provided in the margin) are underlined.

Acts is the book that recounts what the first disciples did in response to God's revelation of Himself in Jesus Christ. In the beginning of the book the disciples are not sure how—or whether—they should act at all. They knew that big changes were coming to their world, but they were unsure of their role in these changes.

1

Ways of Looking at Our Role in Relation to God's

Three different ways of looking at the human role and responsibility for changing the world are:

There are basically three different ways of looking at the human role and responsibility for changing the world. One perspective is: "God isn't going to do anything, so we have to do everything." We might call this the "Tower of Babel" philosophy (Gen. 11). People were worried about being scattered over the face of the earth and losing some of the community and strength that comes through unity. So they acted on their own to build a "tower to heaven" that would serve as a visual rallying point and hold them together. It would also build their egos. With it they would "make a name" for themselves (Gen. 11:4). This philosophy of "we have to do it all ourselves" is not necessarily stated as such, but it drives most human endeavors. Science has done great things for human progress. But some look to it to "save" us from all of our problems, as the Tower of Babel was to do for that era. But science can just as quickly destroy us as save us. We need only look at the tremendous buildup of nuclear, chemical, and biological weaponry to recognize this reality.

The disciples who were present when Christ ascended to heaven were not likely to believe the idea that "God isn't going to do anything so we have to do everything." They had seen God raise Christ from the dead. But they were tempted to believe a second way of looking at our human role, namely that: "God will do everything, so we don't have to do anything." Jesus had spent three years teaching and training them to take over. After it was all over, how did they react?—they stood around gazing at the heavens (vv. 10-11), waiting to see what Jesus was going to do next. They didn't seem to understand that "what happens next" required their participation.

This leads to a third philosophy about the human role in relation to God and how God is changing the world: "God will act, and an important part of His action will be what He does through *us*." Jesus had tried to impress this approach on the disciples all along (Mark 9:14-19; Luke 10:1-20; John 14:12). In the passage from John in particular, Jesus makes the astounding promise that His disciples will be able to do even greater things than He Himself had done—if they act in His name. In reality, the Book of Acts is the story of how Jesus *began* to fulfill that promise.

The Book of Acts is the story of how Jesus began to fulfill what promise?

today's session (cont'd)

Let's look more closely at the Scripture itself and examine what Jesus is teaching the disciples about what is going to happen, and what they need to be doing to help make it happen.

Why did Jesus want the disciples to wait for the gift of the Holy Spirit?

In verse 4, we find that Jesus had told them to "wait [in Jerusalem] for the gift my Father promised." This might have been misunderstood by the disciples to mean that they were just to wait around while God acted. In reality, God was telling them to wait *until God empowered and directed them to act*. This He was about to do through the sending of the Holy Spirit (Acts 2). While God wants us to act, sometimes it is appropriate to wait until God's power and direction comes. Isaiah 40:31 reminds us,

"... but those who wait for the Lord shall renew their
strength;
they shall mount up with wings like eagles,
they shall run and not be weary;
they shall walk and not faint" (NRSV).

In verse 6, the disciples' passive mindset comes out once more. They ask Jesus when *He* is going to "restore the kingdom to Israel." But then in verse 8, He answers by telling them what *they* would be doing by the Holy Spirit's power. Once again, He was trying to help them see that they had a role in establishing God's kingdom.

Expanding the Mission

How did Jesus seek to expand the disciples' view of what their mission was?

Jesus' answer is also more inclusive as far as the mission described. The disciples talked of restoring Israel—Jesus responded with a mission that would start in Jerusalem and then go to "the ends of the earth." The Jews believed that the Messiah (Christ) would restore Israel to its "glory days" under King David. Israel had been under the rule of five successive countries (Assyria, Babylonia, Persia, Greece, and Rome). This covered a period of over seven hundred years of foreign domination. No wonder they were looking for a little political freedom. But Christ wanted them to understand that the freedom He offered was much more extensive. He had come to bring *spiritual* freedom, freedom from sin, guilt, and death, and to bring it to *all* people.

In verse 11, Jesus ascends into heaven and the disciples stand there looking up after Him. This is somewhat of a natural reaction, but God wanted to discourage them from making a habit of it. So He sent an angel to say, "Men of Galilee, why do you stand here looking into the sky? This same Jesus, who has been taken from you into heaven, will come back in the same way you have seen him go into heaven" (v. 11). At first glance, this could be seen as an encouragement to keep on doing what they were doing. Wouldn't they want to keep their eyes open for his return? But the implication of the angel's statement was, "... and you need to be ready for Him!"

What parable of Jesus is cited to illustrate what we should be doing while waiting for Christ to return?

Here we are reminded of a teaching of Jesus recorded in Matthew 24:42-51. He said, "Therefore keep watch, because you do not know on what day your Lord will come." He then tells a parable to illustrate what we should be doing: "Who then is the faithful and wise servant, whom the master has put in charge of his servants in his household to give them their food at the proper time? It will be good for that servant whose master finds him doing so when he returns."

1

What we need to learn from this story in Acts is that we are not called to stand around passively waiting for Christ's return. We are called to be actively sharing the gospel and loving the people around us.

notes:

Remain in groups of 6–8 people, in a horseshoe configuration.

In this small-group session, students will be applying the lessons of the text to their own lives through the following questions.

The students were asked (in the student book) to choose an answer for each question and explain why.

Learning from the Story (5-7 minutes)

1. What "convincing proofs" (v. 3) have you seen that Jesus Christ really is alive?

2. In verse 8, Jesus says "you will be my witnesses." Where do you feel most called to witness for Christ?

   - ☐ to my family members
   - ☐ to my co-workers
   - ☐ to people in my neighborhood
   - ☐ to people in the "Third World"
   - ☐ none of the above—The whole idea of witnessing scares me to death!
   - ☐ other: ______________________

3. How much power do you feel you are getting from the Holy Spirit right now?

   - ☐ not enough to keep a smoke detector from "chirping"
   - ☐ maybe enough to put a weak beam on a flashlight, but that's about it
   - ☐ enough to run a child's toy—The Energizer Bunny would be proud!
   - ☐ enough to run a major home appliance
   - ☐ enough to supply the energy needs for a small city

notes:

Share with the class the following thoughts on how the lessons of this text might be applied today. The answers to the student book questions (provided in the margin) are underlined unless the question requires a personal answer.

In what two ways can the vision of your mission get out of balance?

Where can you find a list of missionaries with whom you might correspond?

life change lessons (5-7 minutes)

1

Jesus was trying to expand the disciples' vision of who was to be included in the kingdom of God. We similarly need to expand the vision of our mission. We can get out of balance in two ways. <u>Some people won't support overseas missions because they say</u>, "<u>We should take care of the people close to home first</u>." <u>Others fail to help the wounded souls of their own family and friends while trying to win the lost in Bangladesh</u>. But Jesus calls us to both a local witness (in Jerusalem) and a wider witness (to the ends of the earth).

In applying today's lesson to our mission, we need to maintain this balance between local and wider witness. Specifically, we should:

1. ADOPT A MISSIONARY. <u>Your church should have a list of missionaries they support</u>. Find one in an area of the world where you have an interest, or one who seems to have a lot in common with you. Start corresponding with this person, and send regular financial support.

2. VISIT A LOCAL MINISTRY. This might be a ministry for feeding or housing homeless people, a ministry that witnesses to victims of drug or alcohol abuse, a youth outreach, or any ministry of interest to you. Learn how they operate and what special needs for support they might have.

3. SPEND SOME TIME IN CONVERSATION WITH A NON-CHRISTIAN ACQUAINTANCE OR LOVED ONE. This should include listening to and hearing this person's concerns. After hearing those concerns, how does the gospel address those concerns? Help them see that connection.

notes:

student book, p. 12

CARING TIME
Remain in groups of 6–8 people, in a horseshoe configuration.

Hand out the Prayer/ Praise Report to the entire group. Ask each subgroup to pray for the empty chair. Pray specifically for God to guide you to someone to bring next week to fill that chair.

After a sufficient time of prayer in subgroups, close in a corporate prayer. Say, "Next week we will talk about: 'Power from Above.' "

Remind participants of the daily Scripture readings and reflective questions found on page 15.

Caring Time (15-20 minutes)

This is the time to develop and express your care for each other. Begin by having each group member finish the sentence:

"The area of my life where I really need the guidance of the Holy Spirit is ..."

Pray for these concerns and any others that are listed on the Prayer/Praise Report. Include prayer for the empty chair.

If you would like to pray silently, say "Amen" when you have finished your prayer, so that the next person will know when to start.

notes:

BIBLE STUDY NOTES

Reference Notes

Use these notes to gain further understanding of the text as you study on your own:

ACTS 1:1
the new command

my former book. That is, the Gospel of Luke. Church tradition is unanimous in its witness that Luke authored both works.
Theophilus. An unknown figure.
all that Jesus began to do and to teach. This is a clue to the way one should view this book—it is the continuing story of the work of Jesus through His Spirit in the life of His body, the church.

ACTS 1:2
the Holy Sprit

until the day he was taken up to heaven. See Luke 24:50-53. The ascension does not mark the end of Jesus' ministry, but simply a new phase of His work. He now exercises his divine reign from heaven.

1

ACTS 1:2
the Holy Sprit
(cont'd)

through the Holy Spirit. The Spirit played an important part in the earthly ministry of Jesus (in His conception—Luke 1:35; in His presentation—Luke 2:25-28; as a summary of His purpose—Luke 3:16; in His baptism—Luke 3:22; in His temptation—Luke 4:1; in His teaching—Luke 4:14; in His prayer; and in His expectations for the future—Luke 24:49).
apostles. See Luke 6:12-16. Apostles were ambassadors especially commissioned to represent the one in whose name they were sent.

ACTS 1:3
the reign of God

In the Gospel, Luke went to some length to underscore the reality of the physical resurrection of Jesus so that his readers could be assured the apostles were not seeing a ghost (Luke 24:37-42). However, he did not mention the span of time over which the appearances occurred. Matthew and John record a couple of these later appearances prior to the ascension.
the kingdom of God. The announcement of the reign of God through which He saves His people was the theme of Jesus' earthly ministry as well (Luke 4:43).

ACTS 1:4–5
the Spirit of God

the gift my Father promised. This gift is the Holy Spirit. (See Isa. 32:15; Joel 2:28-32; Luke 11:13; 12:12; 24:49; Gal. 3:14.) Jesus quotes the words of John the Baptist (Luke 3:16) as a reminder that from the very beginning the expectation was that through Him the Spirit of God would be poured out on all His people.
baptized with the Holy Spirit. Baptism was associated with cleansing. The metaphor would communicate a being flooded with God's Spirit. Thus, Jesus raised the expectations of the disciples regarding what the next step in His agenda for them might be.

ACTS 1:8
the spread of the gospel

This verse embraces the twin themes of the whole book. The mission of Jesus is continued through the work of His Spirit empowering and enabling the disciples to bear witness to Him (Matt. 28:19-20; Luke 12:11-12). The result of this empowering will be the spread of the gospel throughout the world—from the spiritual heart of Israel (Jerusalem), to the immediate vicinity (Judea), to the despised Samaritans in the adjacent province to the north, to the outermost reaches of the earth. The book of Acts is built around these geographical markers. Chapters 1:1–6:7 occur in Jerusalem and Judea; 6:8–8:40 deals with events that lead the church to Samaria; and 9:1 on recounts the chain of events that leads Paul to journey throughout much of the Roman Empire with the good news of Jesus.

ACTS 1:9

a cloud hid him from their sight. This is not a statement of weather conditions at the time, but a declaration of Jesus' deity. See also Daniel 7:13-14.

ACTS 1:11
the return of Jesus

The Mount of Olives, where the ascension occurred (v. 12), was just outside of the city. The angels' message picks up on Zechariah 14:4, which teaches that the Messiah will one day appear on a mountain when He comes to fully establish His reign.

Session

2

Power from Above

Prepare for the Session

	READINGS	REFLECTIVE QUESTIONS
Monday	Acts 2:1–4	How has the Holy Spirit been at work in your life?
Tuesday	Acts 2:5–13	What has God done recently that amazed you?
Wednesday	Acts 2:22–23	How would you like to thank God for what He did for you through the death of His Son Jesus Christ?
Thursday	Acts 2:29–32	Consider how Christ's victory over death has affected your own feelings about your mortality. Does fear of death keep you from fully living your life?
Friday	Acts 2:36–38	Because of what Christ has done for you, what should you be doing for Him?
Saturday	Acts 2:39	Consider how well are you conveying the good news of Jesus Christ to the next generation—to your own children or to nephews, nieces, or children in your sphere of influence?
Sunday	Acts 2:40–41	What might God be warning you about right now in your life? How responsive are you to warnings?

notes:

OUR GOALS FOR THIS SESSION ARE:

In groups of 6–8, gather people in a horseshoe configuration.

Make sure everyone has a name tag.

Take time to share information on class parties that are coming up as well as any relevant church events.

INTRODUCE THE ICEBREAKER ACTIVITY: The students have been told in their books to choose one answer.

After the Icebreaker say something like, "On the day of Pentecost, what got the disciples 'fired up' was the Holy Spirit. What happened then and how it affected the growth of the church is a vital matter, and we will be looking today at what it means for us in the church today."

Hand out the Prayer/Praise Report. A sample copy is on pages 158-159. Have people write down prayer requests and praises. Then have the prayer coordinator collect the report and make copies for use during the Caring Time.

BIBLE STUDY
- to gain a better understanding of what happened when the Holy Spirit came at Pentecost
- to appreciate the power of the Spirit to bring diverse peoples together
- to consider how the Holy Spirit empowers the church today

LIFE CHANGE
- to pray for the Holy Spirit's presence and power
- to commit one day to following the Holy Spirit's guidance
- to encourage our church in one new venture of faith

Icebreaker (10-15 minutes)

Fired Up. Check which of each of the following pairs is most likely to get you "fired up."

a powerful sermon . . . . a powerful song

rock music . . . . a marching band

an appeal to my compassionate side . . . . an appeal to my competitive side

a story of injustice . . . . a story of romance

praise hymns . . . . a dramatic, traditional hymn

notes:

LEARNING FROM THE BIBLE

ACTS 2:1-13

Have a member of the class, selected ahead of time, read the passage from Acts.

Bible Study (30-45 minutes)

The Scripture for this week:

*[1]When the day of Pentecost came, they were all together in one
place. [2]Suddenly a sound like the blowing of a violent wind came
from heaven and filled the whole house where they were sitting. [3]They
saw what seemed to be tongues of fire that separated and came to rest
on each of them. [4]All of them were filled with the Holy Spirit and
began to speak in other tongues as the Spirit enabled them.*

*[5]Now there were staying in Jerusalem God-fearing Jews from
every nation under heaven. [6]When they heard this sound, a crowd
came together in bewilderment, because each one heard them speaking in his own language. [7]Utterly amazed, they asked: "Are not all
these men who are speaking Galileans? [8]Then how is it that each of
us hears them in his own native language? [9]Parthians, Medes and
Elamites; residents of Mesopotamia, Judea and Cappadocia, Pontus
and Asia, [10]Phrygia and Pamphylia, Egypt and the parts of Libya
near Cyrene; visitors from Rome [11](both Jews and converts to
Judaism); Cretans and Arabs—we hear them declaring the wonders
of God in our own tongues!" [12]Amazed and perplexed, they asked one
another, "What does this mean?"*

*[13]Some, however, made fun of them and said, "They have had too
much wine."*

notes:

Summarize these introductory remarks. Be sure to include the underlined information, which gives the answers to the student book questions (provided in the margin).

What question do we need to ask of the church if it is not "working" properly?

...about today's session (5 minutes)

PLUGGED INTO THE SPIRIT

When appliance repair people are called to fix some appliance that is not working, their experience often teaches them to ask one question before they come out—"<u>Are you sure it's plugged in</u>?" That is a question we need to ask of the church if *it* is not working. A church must be "plugged in" to the power of the Holy Spirit if it is to function properly with full power. A church that disregards the power of the Holy Spirit is cutting off its power source.

Finding and supplying sources of power for our country is the cause of much discussion and political wrangling. We are not a nation that can afford to run out of power. Similarly, the church is not a body that can afford to run out of power. Changing the lives of people enslaved to destructive sins and habits, helping bring about justice and peace in an unjust, violent world—these are not tasks we can do under our own power. Only the Holy Spirit's power, working through us, can bring changes of this magnitude. That is why we must learn more about the Spirit's coming, and how we need the presence of the Holy Spirit in our lives and churches today.

What promise is God fulfilling in our passage for today?

In the Scripture passage we looked at last week, the disciples were told, "But you will receive power when the Holy Spirit comes on you ..." (1:8). The passage we will look at this week is God's fulfillment of the promise made in that passage.

notes:

Remain in groups of 6–8 people, in a horseshoe configuration.

In this small-group session, students will be responding to the following questions that will help them share their stories in terms of the coming of the Holy Spirit at Pentecost as described in Acts 2:1-13.

Have the students explore these questions together.

Identifying with the Story (5-7 minutes)

1. When have you had an experience in a group that was so amazing and unique you had a hard time explaining it to people who weren't there?
   - ☐ at a camp or a conference
   - ☐ at a concert
   - ☐ at a sporting event
   - ☐ on a trip
   - ☐ at a very special worship service
   - ☐ other: ____________________
2. With what other cultures have you had contact? Were the relationships between the cultures in your neighborhood or town relaxed or tense?
3. What adult do you remember who really "spoke your language" when you were an adolescent?

today's session (15-20 minutes)

Share with your class the following information which you may modify according to your own perspectives and teaching needs. The answers to the student book questions (provided in the margin) are underlined.

The events of the second chapter of Acts make up what is considered to be the birthday of the church. From this moment forward the Holy Spirit was the driving force behind what became the church's phenomenal expansion throughout the Middle East and Europe. To understand this growth we should carefully study this chapter.

What was the importance of Pentecost before it became the birthday of the church?

In this story, the disciples had come together for Pentecost. Christians sometimes get the mistaken impression that Pentecost has always been a day important only to Christians. However, it is celebrated in the Old Testament fifty days after the Passover. It has been called the "Feast of Weeks," and is celebrated at the end of the grain harvest, much like our Thanksgiving. By New Testament times it also celebrated God's giving of the Law to Moses.

The Wind of the Spirit

***What three different English words translate the Hebrew word* rhuah *and the Greek word* pneuma?**

In verse 2 we read, "Suddenly a sound like the blowing of a violent wind came from heaven and filled the whole house where they were sitting." In both Hebrew (the language in which the Old Testament was originally written) and Greek (the language in which the New Testament was originally written), the word translated as "Spirit" and "wind" and "breath" is all the same word. In Hebrew the word is *rhuah*. In Greek the word is *pneuma*. While one might think that this could lead to confusion, it also adds meaning. Is this "wind" from heaven truly a wind or is it the Spirit of God? Actually, it's both. Similarly when God breathed into humankind the "breath" of life (Gen. 2:7), was it really the "breath" of life or the "Spirit" of life? Again, it was both.

What phrases does the Old Testament use to refer to the Holy Spirit?

When the Holy Spirit came into the room on this Pentecost, was this something entirely new? Not exactly. The Holy Spirit is part of God, and hence was not something invented or created at Pentecost. The Old Testament refers to the Holy Spirit, generally referring to "the Spirit of God" or "the Spirit of the Lord." (See, for instance, Gen. 1:2 and Ezek. 37:1.) What was new at this Pentecost was that the Spirit would now be available to the church of Jesus Christ on a continuing basis.

An Uncontrollable Force Unleashed

What two uncontrollable forces are used to represent the Holy Spirit in this passage?

Note also that it was a *violent* wind that came at Pentecost. What does this description say to us? It reminds us that while the Holy Spirit can bring peace to the soul, the Spirit is also a powerful force that we cannot expect to control or stifle. Even today violent winds like tornadoes and hurricanes frustrate human efforts at controlling them. Human power is humbled by such violent power. Similarly, we note how the tongues that rested on each of the disciples were "as of fire." Fire is also used elsewhere to speak of God's presence (Ex. 3:1-6; Heb. 12:28-29). John the Baptist had spoken of a baptism "with the Holy Spirit and with fire" (Luke 3:16). Firefighters will attest that, like a violent wind, fire is a force that is difficult to control. The church must *experience* the power of the Holy Spirit. The Holy Spirit is to lead us—we are not to try to direct the Spirit where and when to appear.

The church must _________ the power of the Holy Spirit.

2

A Multicultural Community Formed

The "speaking in other tongues" referred to in verse 4 is speaking in other human languages. As such this story is a kind of "reverse tower of Babel" (Gen. 11:1-9). In that story people had tried to bring themselves together as one by building a tower under their own initiative and power. God responded by confusing their language, which drove them apart. Now, at Pentecost, God reverses the process. By miraculously helping everyone to understand one another's language, God brings people together in one Christian experience of faith and worship.

The events of this passage are a reverse of what Old Testament story?

In this story then we see that right from the first, Christ's kingdom was multicultural. There were no "English only" equivalents here. God wanted everyone to understand what was happening in terms of the language with which they were familiar. The gospel was too important a message to become garbled by a language barrier.

We note in verse 5 that "God-fearing Jews from every nation" were present during this experience. This was made possible because the Feast of Weeks (Pentecost) was a time when Jews would come from everywhere to celebrate. What an appropriate time to initiate a church in which all peoples become one in Christ. Wonders Accomplished

Verse 11 speaks of "the wonders of God" that the people there all witnessed. The result was that people were "amazed" (vv. 7,12) and "perplexed" (v. 12)—anything but "bored." What happens when churches lose the Holy Spirit? Some imply that churches where the people show less emotion have lost the Spirit. But that is not necessarily the case. The best evidence of the Holy Spirit's presence is not emotional expression (although in some people the Spirit's presence does result in emotional expression), but the manifestation of acts of God's power. This means we need to be open to letting God do great things through us. And God can only do great things through us if we act in faith for God. It's not going to happen if we play it safe. Christian researcher George Barna, in writing about what successful churches today do and don't do, says, "Growing

God can only do great things through us if we _______ ____ _________ for God.

today's session (cont'd)

churches got to where they were because they were willing to take measured risks. They were willing to do some unusual things, to demonstrate creativity in their approach to reaching people. They generally understood that to be safe in ministry is to be stifled. To make gains, a church must take some risks."[1] Thus a church that wants the Spirit to do great things through them needs to reach out and attempt bigger things than they might think they could accomplish on their own.

The end result of the events of Pentecost Sunday was that three thousand people came to faith in Jesus Christ (2:41). The number of converts is not the only indicator of the presence of the Holy Spirit. There are also people who are cared for in the name of Jesus Christ, the poor and oppressed are stood up for (Luke 4:16-21), and the "seed" of the gospel is spread (Matt. 13:1-23).

notes:

Remain in groups of 6–8 people, in a horseshoe configuration.

In this small-group session, students will be applying the lessons of the text to their own lives through the following questions.

The students were asked (in the student book) to choose an answer for each question and explain why.

Learning from the Story (5-7 minutes)

1. Had you been present when the Holy Spirit came upon the disciples at Pentecost, who would you have been more like—those who were amazed by the wonders of God, or those who thought the disciples were drunk? Mark where you would be on the scale below.

1 · · · · · · · · · · 2 · · · · · · · · · · 3 · · · · · · · · · · 4 · · · · · · · · · · 5

those who were amazed — those who thought them drunk

2. What do you feel you most need the power of the Holy Spirit to do in your life right now?

- ▢ to help me connect with others, as when the "cultural gap" was bridged at Pentecost
- ▢ to help me learn more of "the wonders of God"
- ▢ to help me be used to share "the wonders of God"
- ▢ other: ______________________________

3. If you were to share just one "wonder of God" that you have experienced, what would it be?

Share with the class the following thoughts on how the lessons of this text might be applied today. The answers to the student book questions (provided in the margin) are underlined unless the question requires a personal answer.

What two things must we not do in relation to this study?

What difference do some people see between the church of today and the church of Peter and Paul? How accurate is that perception?

life change lessons (5-7 minutes)

How do we plug ourselves and our churches into this power source called the Holy Spirit? That is the practical question of this chapter. There are two things we must not do in relation to our study. One is to look at Acts simply as an historical document, telling us about the past. In a real sense, it is a document about what the church must be *today*. The second thing we must not do, and it's related to the first, is to think that the early church was qualitatively different than the church today. Some people imply that we cannot expect to do what was done in Acts because that church was made up of "saints" like Peter and Paul, and we are mere human beings. But Peter and Paul were human beings just as we are (Acts 14:15). The power behind what they did was the power of the Holy Spirit, a power that is also made available to us. Therefore we need to act on what we have learned by:

life change lessons (cont'd)

1. PRAYING FOR THE HOLY SPIRIT'S PRESENCE AND POWER. This is a simple action, but it is an essential one. Jesus has told us that in order to have this power, we must ask for it (Luke 11:9-13).

2. COMMITTING ONE DAY TO FOLLOWING THE HOLY SPIRIT'S GUIDANCE. Set this day aside in advance and commit yourself to following the guidance of the Holy Spirit wherever He might lead you for that entire day. See what this experience says to you about the Spirit's role in the rest of your life.

3. ENCOURAGING YOUR CHURCH IN ONE NEW VENTURE OF FAITH. This should be a ministry that your church has never done before, and one that stretches the people of your church to reach beyond what they could do on their own.

notes:

CARING TIME
Remain in groups of 6–8 people, in a horseshoe configuration.

Hand out the Prayer/Praise Report to the entire group. Ask each subgroup to pray for the empty chair. Pray specifically for God to guide you to someone to bring next week to fill that chair.

After a sufficient time of prayer in subgroups, close in a corporate prayer. Say, "Next week we will talk about: 'A New Kind of Community.' "

Remind participants of the daily Scripture readings and reflective questions found on page 23.

Caring Time (15-20 minutes)

During this prayer time, thank God for the "wonders of God" that group members have experienced in their lives. Take turns praying for each other, asking for the Holy Spirit's presence and power to fill each person's life and ministry. Also, use the Prayer/Praise Report and pray for the concerns listed.

Close by praying specifically for God to guide you to someone to invite for next week to fill the empty chair.

notes:

BIBLE STUDY NOTES

Reference Notes

Use these notes to gain further understanding of the text as you study on your own:

ACTS 2:1
Feast of Weeks

the day of Pentecost. This was the Feast of Weeks (Ex. 23:16; Lev. 23:15-21; Deut. 16:9-12) held fifty days after Passover. Originally a kind of Thanksgiving Day for gathered crops, it came to be associated with the commemoration of the giving of the Law at Sinai (Ex. 20:1-17). Jewish tradition held that when God gave the Law to Moses, a single voice spoke that was heard by all the nations of the world in their own language. Luke may be alluding to that in this story. Pentecost was a celebration which thousands of Jews from all over the empire would attend.

ACTS 2:2–4
wind and fire

The Greek word for "wind" and "spirit" is the same, hence the symbolism of the Spirit coming like a great wind. Fire is often associated with divine appearances (Ex. 3:2; 19:18). John the Baptist said Jesus would baptize His followers with the Holy Spirit and fire (Luke 3:16), symbolizing the cleansing, purifying effect of the Spirit. What is important here is that tongues served as a sign to the crowds of a supernatural event, the point of which was Jesus Christ.

ACTS 2:4
baptism

filled with the Holy Spirit. This phrase is found elsewhere (Acts 4:8,31; 13:52; Eph. 5:18) indicating a repeatable experience. Here, however, it is clearly associated with the baptism of the Spirit (Acts 1:5), which is an experience new converts enter into upon acceptance of Jesus as the Messiah (Acts 2:41).

ACTS 2:5–8

The disciples apparently made their way to the temple where they attracted a large crowd that was puzzled over how they could speak in their native dialects.

ACTS 2:9–11
international community

Parthians, Medes and Elamites ... Mesopotamia. Present-day Iran and Iraq, to the east of Jerusalem. These Jews traced their roots back to the Assyrian overthrow of Israel and the Babylonian overthrow of Judea seven and five centuries beforehand respectively.

Judea. Either the immediate environs around Jerusalem is in view, or Luke is thinking of the days under David and Solomon when the land of Israel stretched from Egypt on the west to the Euphrates River on the east.

Cappadocia, Pontus and Asia, Phrygia and Pamphylia. Present-day Turkey to the north of Jerusalem. Much of Acts takes place in this region.

Egypt ... Libya near Cyrene. To the west of Jerusalem on the northern coast of Africa.

converts to Judaism. Judaism's high morality and developed spirituality attracted many Gentiles in other religions.

Cretans. An island south of Greece in the Mediterranean Sea.

Arabs. The Nabetean kingdom was south of Jerusalem with borders on Egypt and the Euphrates.

[1] George Barna, *User Friendly Churches* (Ventura, CA: Regal Books, 1991) pp. 182–183.

Session

3 A New Kind of Community

Prepare for the Session

	READINGS	REFLECTIVE QUESTIONS
Monday	Acts 2:42–45	How are you ministering to the needs of the believers around you?
Tuesday	Acts 2:46–47	Can you honestly say that you have a glad heart at this point in your life? If not, why not?
Wednesday	Acts 3:2–7	What do you have that you can give others in the name of Jesus Christ? How generously are you giving this?
Thursday	Acts 3:9–10	How might people see you as being changed because of the way Christ has touched you?
Friday	Acts 3:16	What weaknesses do you have that need to be made strong by Jesus Christ? Are you trusting God to strengthen them?
Saturday	Acts 3:19–20	What is God calling you to repent of right now?
Sunday	Acts 4:1–20	Do you feel the same compulsion that Peter and John felt to share what Christ has done for you? If not, why not?

notes:

OUR GOALS FOR THIS SESSION ARE:

In groups of 6–8, gather people in a horseshoe configuration.

Make sure everyone has a name tag.

Take time to share information on class parties that are coming up as well as any relevant church events.

INTRODUCE THE ICEBREAKER ACTIVITY: The students have been told in their books to choose one answer.

After the Icebreaker, say something like, "While we all have a variety of activities that we do with others, a mark of the early church as described in Acts was that they really enjoyed doing virtually everything together. This strong fellowship was part of what attracted others. We will look today at how this happened."

Hand out the Prayer/Praise Report. A sample copy is on pages 158-159. Have people write down prayer requests and praises. Then have the prayer coordinator collect the report and make copies for use during the Caring Time.

BIBLE STUDY	• to look at the nature of the community of the early church • to determine what factors made the early church so effective • to see how emulating certain qualities of the early church might make today's churches more powerful
LIFE CHANGE	• to find one new way we can minister to each other's needs • to invite others over to our homes • to work together on a class covenant

Icebreaker (10-15 minutes)

It's Better Together. Go around the group on question 1 and let everyone share. Then go around on question 2.

1. Which of the following activities would you rather do with friends? Which would you prefer to do alone? Mark those you prefer to do with friends with an "F," and mark those you prefer to do alone with an "A."

___ eating lunch or dinner
___ watching television
___ going to a sporting event
___ fishing
___ driving on a long trip
___ shopping
___ worshiping God

2. Pick one of the activities you said you prefer to do with friends. What is the most important quality you look for in someone with whom to do this activity?

☐ similar interests
☐ easy to talk to
☐ good sense of humor
☐ empathetic
☐ nonjudgmental
☐ someone I can be myself with
☐ a good listener
☐ strong moral values

notes:

LEARNING FROM THE BIBLE

ACTS 2:42-47

Have one member of the class, selected ahead of time, lead the class in reading the passage from Acts.

Bible Study (30-45 minutes)

The Scripture for this week:

*[42]They devoted themselves to the apostles' teaching and to the fel-
lowship, to the breaking of bread and to prayer. [43]Everyone was filled
with awe, and many wonders and miraculous signs were done by the
apostles. [44]All the believers were together and had everything in common. [45]Selling their possessions and goods, they gave to anyone as he had
need. [46]Every day they continued to meet together in the temple courts.
They broke bread in their homes and ate together with glad and sincere hearts, [47]praising God and enjoying the favor of all the people. And
the Lord added to their number daily those who were being saved.*

notes:

Summarize these introductory remarks. Be sure to include the underlined information, which gives the answers to the student book questions (provided in the margin).

What is one example of a product that might be developed from a prototype?

What does it mean to make the church of Acts a prototype for churches today?

...about today's session (5 minutes)

A CHURCH PROTOTYPE

When a company develops a new product, like a new model of car, they first build a prototype. This shows how the new model can perform and what it needs to look like, and serves as a model from which to build the other cars to follow. Similarly, the church that was built in Jerusalem during the infancy of the Christian faith can be seen as a prototype for churches down through the ages. That doesn't mean that every church needs to function exactly like the church as it is described in Acts. (For instance, most churches will not have "everything in common.") However, it does mean we can learn some important elements that ought to be present in every church and its ministry. There is no better passage for studying these elements than the one we will be looking at today (along with its parallel passage in Acts 4:32-37). It is a summary statement for what the common life of the church was like at this time.

In looking at this early church, we don't want to over-idealize it. Like all churches, this one also had problems (Acts 6 will deal with one of them). However, in our session we will concentrate on understanding this church's strengths, in the hope that those strengths can also be claimed by the churches of which we are a part today.

Remain in groups of 6–8 people, in a horseshoe configuration.

In this small-group session, students will be responding to the following questions that will help them share their stories in terms of the early church.

Have the students explore these questions together.

Identifying with the Story (5-7 minutes)

1. When have you experienced a fellowship like these believers had together?

   - ☐ with a group of high school friends
   - ☐ with a group of college friends
   - ☐ at a conference where everyone got really close
   - ☐ with a church small group
   - ☐ never
   - ☐ other: ________________________________

2. Which of the factors present in this story is most important to you in developing fellowship with other believers? Rank them in order from "1" (most important) to "6" (least important):

   ___ devotion to common teaching and belief (v. 42)
   ___ praying together (v. 42)
   ___ doing exciting, wondrous works together (v. 43)
   ___ caring for each other's physical, emotional, and spiritual needs (vv. 44-45)
   ___ regular, common worship that includes praising God (vv. 46--7)
   ___ doing everyday things together, like eating and being in each other's homes (v. 46)

3. Which of the factors listed in question 2 is missing most in your present relationships with other believers?

notes:

Share with your class the following information which you may modify according to your own perspectives and teaching needs. The answers to the student book questions (provided in the margin) are underlined.

today's session (15-20 minutes)

Last week we looked at the coming of the Holy Spirit at Pentecost. The passage we are considering today is another vital part of this most important chapter. It basically underlines both the "miraculous signs" and the kind of community that was created by the amazing events on that Pentecost.

Church Growth in the Early Church

How often were people saved in the church described in this passage?

Starting at the end, we read that "the Lord added to their number daily those who were being saved" (v. 47). Since most churches today, at least those in the most economically privileged sections of Western civilization, don't come close to achieving this kind of success in evangelism, we need to examine what caused this growth. To begin, let's look at what preceded this verse. In verse 43 we read that "many wonders and miraculous signs were done." To understand some particulars of this we can look at Acts 5:12,15-16:

> *The apostles performed many miraculous signs and wonders among the people. And all the believers used to meet together in Solomon's Colonnade . ... As a result, people brought the sick into the streets and laid them on beds and mats so that at least Peter's shadow might fall on some of them as he passed by. Crowds gathered also from the towns around Jerusalem, bringing their sick and those tormented by evil spirits, and all of them were healed.*

What were some of the "wonders and miraculous signs" being done by the apostles?

A Ministry of Healing

Just like Jesus' healing ministry created a buzz among the populace (Mark 1:40-45; John 6:1-2), so also did the healing ministry of the early church. We debate back and forth between various denominations and Christian perspectives whether this kind of miraculous healing ministry can be done in the church of today. Rather than debating, we should be focusing on need fulfillment. In the early church, medicine was not nearly as advanced as it is today, so this healing ministry was filling a desperate need that the people had. What similar needs do people have today that the church can address? What can we be doing to respond to human need that would bring the people to us in the same manner this healing ministry brought people to the early church? How can we tap the power of God in responding to such need? These are the questions we must answer. In some cases, the answer may be in a healing ministry. Even modern medicine does not understand why people sometimes miraculously recover. Faith and prayer often seem to be the only answer. Other churches may turn more to helping with a

What are some of the human needs to which today's church might respond?

different kind of recovery—recovery from alcohol or drug addiction. Recovery programs with a spiritual basis consistently prove more effective than medical or secular approaches. Still other churches might concentrate on emotional or relational needs like loneliness, help in parenting and grandparenting, or dealing with life stresses.

Responding jointly to human need is an important key. In verse 44, we read that the disciples, "were together and had everything in common." This was a primitive form of socialism, but certainly without the totalitarianism we associate with it today. While one might question the political practicality of this approach, the attitude behind it was exemplary. The people decided to take the attitude, "Your need is my need." Then they gave caring to each other that went beyond smiles and well-wishing.

What is one contributing factor to the social need experienced in our country?

Much need in modern America is social need. This is, in part, due to a rise in single-person households. In the 1950s, about one in every ten households had only one person. But today, due to the three D's of social statistics (death, divorce, and deferred marriage), about one in every four persons is a single-person household, and this is predicted to rise to one in every three households in the 21st century.[1] In verse 46, we read that the people "continued to meet together in the temple courts. They broke bread in their homes and ate together ... ." These people gave each other the precious gift of their time. In contrast, our society is becoming a more isolated society. People today refer to "cocooning" —going home to the isolated "cocoon" of one's home and not coming out unless they have to (which isn't often, given all that can be done on the Internet). People today are hungry, however, for intimacy and friendship, and that takes time. We need to understand that to get the kind of community they had in the early church, we must invest our time in each other.

Ministry to Spiritual Need

Certainly a primary area of need to which the church must respond is spiritual need. In verse 42 we are told, "They devoted themselves to the apostles' teaching." This reminds us that a true Christian fellowship cannot exist without focusing on a common faith in Jesus Christ. When we have a common understanding of God's love and a passion for Christ, the bonds between us are set even stronger. This is also connected with verse 47, which tells us that the people were "praising God" together. A growing, thriving church must have vital worship.

Ministering to people's spiritual needs might mean bringing healing to what aspects of their lives?

Ministering to spiritual need means bringing healing to people's guilt, their alienation from the rest of creation, and their sense of separation from God, their Creator. This kind of healing cannot be done by psychologists, medical doctors, or social service agencies.

today's session (cont'd)

What is the relationship between religious activity and health, according to a growing number of medical studies?

Spiritual health can affect other areas of life as well. A growing number of medical studies reveal that strongly religious individuals are likely to be healthier and even live longer than less religious people. In fact as of the year 2000, six medical schools were using grants from the John Templeton Foundation to incorporate faith or spirituality into the practice of medical care.2 A church that ministers to spiritual need, in fact, also ministers to the whole person.

And so we see that the church of this time grew because the Holy Spirit empowered them to become a deeply caring community of believers, where God was able to do great deeds. These great deeds were done through a church that cared about human need of every kind, from physical to relational to spiritual. That is the kind of church we should also seek to be.

notes:

Remain in groups of 6–8 people, in a horseshoe configuration.

In this small-group session, students will be applying the lessons of the text to their own lives through the following questions.

The students were asked (in the student book) to choose an answer for each question and explain why.

Learning from the Story (5-7 minutes)

1. How do you relate to the early church's practice of having "everything in common" (v. 44)?

- ☐ It is communistic!
- ☐ It is naive, though well-intentioned.
- ☐ It is the way things should be in the church.
- ☐ I can't see myself ever being part of such a practice.
- ☐ I think I could really get into a community that did this.

2. Which of the factors present in this story do you think most contributed to the result that "the Lord added to their number daily those who were being saved" (v. 47)?

- ☐ devotion to common teaching and belief (v. 42)
- ☐ praying together (v. 42)
- ☐ doing a lot of exciting, wondrous works together (v. 43)
- ☐ caring for each other's physical, emotional, and spiritual needs (vv. 44-45)
- ☐ regular, common worship that includes praising God (vv. 46-47)
- ☐ doing everyday things together, like eating and being in each other's homes (v. 46)

3. Were your church to minister to the greatest need of the people in your community, what need would that be, and what would your church need to "sell" or sacrifice to minister to that need?

notes:

Share with the class the following thoughts on how the lessons of this text might be applied today. The answers to the student book questions (provided in the margin) are underlined unless the question requires a personal answer.

How does the idea of "fellowship" as displayed in this passage of Acts compare to the idea of "fellowship" as many modern churches understand it?

What are some aspects of church life we need to look at in order to truly strengthen church fellowship?

life change lessons (5-7 minutes)

When you talk about "fellowship," in many churches people assume you are talking about one of two activities: The time after worship when they have coffee, punch, and cookies; or their periodic potluck suppers. But as we have looked at this passage in Acts, we see that "fellowship" can be a much more expansive concept than that. Christian fellowship can be an intense sharing that includes responding to each other's needs, celebrating common faith, and sharing life in a far more extensive way than what happens when you gather for worship (and perhaps have coffee afterward).

In order to have the kind of fellowship displayed by the church in Acts, we need to look at the whole of what the church is doing. We need to look at how it does missions, where and in what ways it gathers, and what it does when it is not gathered. More specifically, here are some ways we can accomplish this:

1. FIND ONE NEW WAY THE PEOPLE IN YOUR CLASS CAN MINISTER TO EACH OTHER'S NEEDS. What starts in your class can easily spread to the rest of the church! This can be anything from providing food for class members when a family member dies, to developing a prayer chain, to developing a system of "secret pals" doing little acts of caring for each other.

life change lessons (cont'd)

2. INVITE OTHERS OVER TO YOUR HOME. This might mean inviting other members of the class, or it might mean the class inviting other church members, visitors, or members of another class over to their homes. There are few ways that are more helpful in getting to know each other than spending time in each other's homes. It is there that people see the pictures of those who make up your life, and the style that expresses who you are.

3. WORK TOGETHER ON A CLASS COVENANT. This can be an expression of the central beliefs you hold in common, as well as a promise to each other concerning how you are agreeing to support and care for one another.

notes:

CARING TIME
Remain in groups of 6–8 people, in a horseshoe configuration.

Hand out the Prayer/Praise Report to the entire group. Ask each subgroup to pray for the empty chair. Pray specifically for God to guide you to someone to bring next week to fill that chair.

After a sufficient time of prayer in subgroups, close in a corporate prayer. Say, "Next week we will talk about: 'A New Kind of Community.' "

Remind participants of the daily Scripture readings and reflective questions found on page 31.

Caring Time (15-20 minutes)

Remember that this is the time for expressing your concern for each other as group members and for supporting one another in prayer. Begin by having each group member finish this sentence:

"The area of need where this group could minister to me this week is ..."

Pray for these needs, in addition to the concerns listed on the Prayer/Praise Report. Remember to pray for God's guidance in inviting someone to the group next week to fill the empty chair.

notes:

BIBLE STUDY NOTES

Reference Notes

Use these notes to gain further understanding of the text as you study on your own:

ACTS 2:42
life of the church

The four components of the church's life listed here may represent what occurred at their gatherings.

teaching. The foundation for the church's life was the instruction given by the apostles as the representatives of Jesus.

fellowship. Literally, "sharing." While this may include the aspect of sharing to meet material needs (v. 45), it most likely means their common participation in the Spirit as they worshiped together (1 Cor. 12).

the breaking of bread. The Lord's Supper in which they remembered Jesus' death (Luke 22:19) and recognized His presence among them (Luke 24:30-31).

to prayer. Literally, "the prayers." This may refer to set times and forms of prayer as was the practice of the Jews.

ACTS 2:43–47
fellowship of the church

The picture of the church is one of continual growth (vv. 43,47), marked by generous sharing (vv. 44-45), and joyful worship and fellowship (vv. 46-47). The worship at the temple continued as before since the line dividing Christianity from Judaism had not yet been drawn. Christians simply saw their faith as the natural end of what the Jewish faith had always declared.

ACTS 2:44–45
outreach of the church

everything in common. While this was a primitive form of socialism, it certainly did not include the oppressive totalitarianism or denial of God found in many modern forms. It was simply an outgrowth of the intense love people had for each other through Jesus Christ. They believed that in Christ each person's need becomes everyone's need.

ACTS 2:47
growth of the church

And the Lord added. Growth in the church was a natural result of the love, fellowship, and commitment to the apostle's teaching, which this section describes.

notes:

[1] Kerby Anderson in an article on "Loneliness" (1993) in the website for Probe Ministries at www.probe.org.

[2] Cheryl Tevis, "Religious faith may be good for what ails you," reprinted from *Successful Farming* magazine in find articles.com, copyright 2000, Gale Group.

3

student book, p. 31

Session 4

When Conflict Hits the Church

Prepare for the Session

	READINGS	REFLECTIVE QUESTIONS
Monday	Acts 6:1–7	What special ministry might God be calling you to do in your church or community?
Tuesday	Acts 7:37–43	Consider the false gods around you in the world. Which ones are you tempted to worship?
Wednesday	Acts 7:51–53	How are you stubbornly resisting God's Word for your life right now? What would help you be more open to that Word?
Thursday	Acts 7:57–60	How well are you doing forgiving those who have done harm to you?
Friday	Acts 8:1–8	How has God taken the bad things that have happened to you and used them for good?
Saturday	Acts 8:30–31	What spiritual issues are you having trouble understanding right now? Who might be able to help you with your struggle?
Sunday	Acts 8:36–40	What is the next step God is calling you toward in your Christian growth? How willing are you to take that step?

notes:

OUR GOALS FOR THIS SESSION ARE:

In groups of 6–8, gather people in a horseshoe configuration.

Make sure everyone has a name tag.

Take time to share information on class parties that are coming up as well as any relevant church events.

INTRODUCE THE ICEBREAKER ACTIVITY: The students have been told in their books to choose one answer.

After the Icebreaker, say something like, "Just as we have certain roles in our families, so in the church we all have our different roles to play. In the story we are looking at today, a conflict between two groups of widows resulted in the assignment of people to a new role in the church– that of serving the physical needs of church members. We will look at how this delegation of responsibility worked as a conflict-resolution tactic."

Hand out the Prayer/Praise Report. A sample copy is on pages 158-159. Have people write down prayer requests and praises. Then have the prayer coordinator collect the report and make copies for use during the Caring Time.

BIBLE STUDY
- to examine a conflict situation in the early church and see what we can learn from it
- to consider how tasks were delegated in the early church according to gifts
- to see how conflict is natural and unavoidable even in a church setting

LIFE CHANGE
- to visit with the pastor and several lay people to find out who are the disaffected groups in our church
- to compare the makeup of the governing board or body of our church with the makeup of the congregation as a whole
- to pray for people in our church who have a different perspective or need than us and the groups of which we feel a part

Icebreaker (10-15 minutes)

Myself as an Appliance. In any well-functioning group, different people must take different roles. What is your role in your family? Go around the group on question 1 and let everyone share. Then go around on question 2.

1. If you could compare the role you have taken in your family to a household appliance, what appliance would it be?

   - ☐ the vacuum cleaner—I pick up after everyone.
   - ☐ the washing machine agitator—When things get too calm I stir things up.
   - ☐ the heater—When people come in from the cold world I warm them up.
   - ☐ the television—I'm the entertainer.
   - ☐ the smoke alarm—I keep others alert to dangers.
   - ☐ the thermostat—I keep things comfortable.
   - ☐ the refrigerator—I provide all of the good stuff people seem to want.
   - ☐ the electric screwdriver—I fix things and keep them running.

2. How happy are you with this role right now?

LEARNING FROM THE BIBLE

ACTS 6:1-7

Have a member of the class, selected ahead of time, read the passage from Acts.

Bible Study (30-45 minutes)

The Scripture for this week:

*1 In those days when the number of disciples was increasing, the
Grecian Jews among them complained against the Hebraic Jews
because their widows were being overlooked in the daily distribution
of food. 2 So the Twelve gathered all the disciples together and said,
"It would not be right for us to neglect the ministry of the word of God
in order to wait on tables. 3 Brothers, choose seven men from among
you who are known to be full of the Spirit and wisdom. We will turn
this responsibility over to them 4 and will give our attention to prayer
and the ministry of the word."*

*5 This proposal pleased the whole group. They chose Stephen, a
man full of faith and of the Holy Spirit; also Philip, Procorus,
Nicanor, Timon, Parmenas, and Nicolas from Antioch, a convert to
Judaism. 6 They presented these men to the apostles, who prayed and
laid their hands on them.*

*7 So the word of God spread. The number of disciples in Jerusalem
increased rapidly, and a large number of priests became obedient to
the faith.*

notes:

Summarize these introductory remarks. Be sure to include the underlined information, which gives the answers to the student book questions (provided in the margin).

What examples of modern church conflicts are mentioned here? What examples could you add to the list?

...about today's session (5 minutes)

CHURCH CONFLICT RESOLUTION

Every day we see examples of the conflict and political wrangling that occurs in secular businesses and government organizations. Sometimes when we get really tired of such happenings we turn to the church as a refuge from such conflict. As a "spiritual" organization, we expect to find people who are beyond all of that. But it turns out that's not the way it is. Instead, we find there is political wrangling as various individuals or groups vie for the pastor's attention or even seek to undermine the pastor. We find conflicts between old and young over worship style, and conflicts between "conservatives" and "liberals" over church school curriculum. We may even see conflicts over what color of carpet to order for the church library. Many who see these conflicts are disillusioned and may even leave the church.

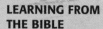

Fill in the blank: "... though the church has a divine commission, it has a decidedly human membership; and where there are human beings, there will be ___________." Do you agree with this statement? Why or why not?

What we need to remember is that even though the church has a divine commission, it has a decidedly human membership; and where there are human beings, there will be conflict. We need to focus on effective ways of handling this conflict. Our Scripture passage today gives us a beautiful example of how to do this. It reminds us that conflict in the church has been there since the very beginning. However, it also shows us that if conflict is handled properly the church can still thrive. If people with a complaint know that their complaint is heard, and if all groups are represented in leadership, then conflict will generally not hobble a church. As we look at this story, we will see how this worked in the church of Acts.

Remain in groups of 6–8 people, in a horseshoe configuration.

In this small-group session, students will be responding to the following questions that will help them share their stories in terms of the conflict in the early church in Acts 6:1-7.

Have the students explore these questions together.

Identifying with the Story (5-7 minutes)

1. What are people in the household where you live most likely to complain about?

   - ☐ nothing to eat in the house
   - ☐ someone else having control of the TV remote
   - ☐ other people's clutter
   - ☐ someone else using the computer
   - ☐ someone else monopolizing the phone
   - ☐ lack of time spent together
   - ☐ respect their personal space
   - ☐ other: ______________________________

2. Which of the following phrases best typifies your approach to dealing with complaints? Is there a difference between how you respond at work and at home?

   - ☐ "Here's the world's smallest violin playing, 'My heart bleeds for you'!"
   - ☐ "It's my way or the highway!"
   - ☐ "You can't please all of the people all of the time."
   - ☐ "You have a right to your opinion."
   - ☐ "File a report and we'll talk."
   - ☐ "It's probably my fault."
   - ☐ "Anything to make you happy."

3. When have you felt like you were "being overlooked" (v. 1) in a church situation?

4

Share with your class the following information which you may modify according to your own perspectives and teaching needs. The answers to the student book questions (provided in the margin) are underlined.

today's session (15-20 minutes)

Sometimes we are tempted to over-idealize the early church, as if it were the perfect Christian fellowship. Certainly when we look at passages like the one we have already studied in Acts 2:42-47 (and its "echo" in Acts 4:32-37), we realize that the fellowship of the early church had a lot going for them. But they had their problems, too, and we will look at how they handled one of those problems in this week's session.

Our passage for today tells us that these events happened "when the number of disciples was increasing" (v. 1). This reminds us that the early church was a fast-growing body. We usually look at church growth as being positive, but it can also bring some conditions that people don't like, such as change and the acceptance of new cultures.

What were some of the differences between Grecian and Hebraic Jews?

In this passage, the conflict is between the Grecian Jews and the Hebraic Jews. The Grecian Jews were followers of Christ, but they were Jews that had lived in and adapted to Greek culture. The Hebraic Jews were Jews who had not made such a cultural adaptation. (We can see such a conflict today in the Arab countries or even Asian countries where some people follow the traditional culture and some are "westernized.") What were some of the areas where these cultures clashed? The more traditional Hebrews would have looked down on every aspect of Greek culture, and hence probably also on the Jews who were influenced by Greek culture. The Hellenists would revere Scripture, but also would have some knowledge of and respect for Greek philosophy. However, what brought such a diverse group of people together at all was Jesus Christ. This made the early church unique, as no other group of the time welcomed differing cultures.

Why was it especially important at this time to take care of the needs of widows?

Still, there were problems. We read that "the Grecian Jews among them complained against the Hebraic Jews because their widows were being overlooked in the daily distribution of food." In Old Testament and New Testament times, it was considered very important to take care of the needs of widows (Ex. 22:22-24; Jas. 1:27). They had no "Social Security." Women didn't have access to most jobs. The church therefore acted to take care of the needs of their widows. The word translated "being overlooked" might have meant that they received less food, or that they received less positive attention when the food was given out.

In order to address this problem, the twelve disciples got together and decided to delegate some duties to a new classification of church leader. The Twelve said, "It would not be right for us to neglect the ministry of the word of God in order to wait on tables." They were not putting down the task of waiting on tables, but simply saying that their gifts and calling meant they needed to be involved in preaching, teaching, and evangelizing. Is one gift "nobler" than other gifts? Paul answers this question in 1 Corinthians 13. He emphasizes that LOVE is the greatest gift—and certainly serving food to needy widows is an act of love. A church that is to be unified and deal constructively with conflict must respect and use all kinds of gifts from all groups of people.

What does Paul say in 1 Corinthians 13 is the greatest gift of all? How does this relate to those who used their gifts to "wait on tables"?

The people chosen to do this task are regarded by some as the first church deacons. It is certainly true that they were chosen to be servant-leaders in the first church. Notice how the names of all of these men are Greek names. Why might that be? The disciples were acting with sensitivity toward their Hellenistic brothers and sisters. Some today might call it "trying to be politically correct." But they were not conscious of political correctness or incorrectness in this choice. Rather they were being conscious of the body of Christ, and the need to keep it one.

Why is it significant that those selected to these positions all had Greek names?

In confronting church conflict today, churches err if they seek to keep all the power in the hands of one group. For instance, church leaders may be persons of retirement age, resulting in younger members being shut out of the decisionmaking. Or a church that has been traditionally made up of persons with a white European background, but which now has a significant number of African-Americans, keeps the old power structure and does not include African-American leaders. In today's society, growing churches often bring in people who are significantly different from those whom they have traditionally served, and this change can bring conflict if such persons are not listened to (as the Twelve listened to the Grecian Jews) and brought into leadership.

When the people were selected for this ministry we are told that the disciples "prayed and laid their hands on them." The laying on of hands is a symbol of the conveying of the Holy Spirit. (See also Acts 13:2-3 and 2 Tim. 1:6). It is most often done today with missionaries and newly ordained pastors, but may also be done with lay ministers. The Holy Spirit empowers the church and binds us together as one. Divisive talk and action grieves the Holy Spirit (Eph. 4:29-32) and destroys the unity of the temple in which the Spirit lives (1 Cor. 3:16-17). Maintaining the unity of the church is hence not just an obligation to each other, but even more is an obligation to God.

Why did the Twelve "lay their hands on" these new church leaders?

Our passage goes on to say that because of the work of people like the Twelve and the servant-leaders they commissioned, "a large number of priests became obedient to the faith" (v. 7). Priests knew the most about sacrifice for sin, and the most spiritually sensitive

today's session (cont'd)

among them no doubt understood that sacrificing an animal was inadequate. Only the sacrifice of the perfect Lamb of God could really atone for sin.

What eventually happened to Stephen?

One of those selected to minister as a servant-leader was Stephen. He went on to include preaching in his ministry as well. That preaching eventually met opposition and got him killed as the first Christian martyr. At his execution a young man named Saul consented to this essentially illegal vigilante act (Acts 7:57–8:1). But the good news is that he later was touched by Christ himself and became known as the Apostle Paul. We will look at his story next week.

notes:

Remain in groups of 6–8 people, in a horseshoe configuration.

In this small-group session, students will be applying the lessons of the text to their own lives through the following questions.

The students were asked (in the student book) to choose an answer for each question and explain why.

Learning from the Story (5-7 minutes)

1. Had you been one of the Twelve, how would you have most likely dealt with this conflict?
   - ☐ I would have told them to file a report.
   - ☐ I would have ignored it and figured it would go away.
   - ☐ I would have written them off as complainers and hoped they would leave the church.
   - ☐ I would have tried to solve the problem directly myself.
   - ☐ I would have delegated the problem to someone qualified, as the Twelve did.

2. Where do you see "cultural clashes" like this one in the church today? What needs to be done to get past cultural differences and encourage a fellowship that cares for one another?

3. Who is being neglected in your church today? What can you do to correct that situation?

life change lessons (5-7 minutes)

Share with the class the following thoughts on how the lessons of this text might be applied today. The answers to the student book questions (provided in the margin) are underlined unless the question requires a personal answer.

Why is dropping out or leaving a church in conflict often an unhealthy option?

Now that we have seen what was done to resolve conflict in the church of Acts, what should we do when similar conflicts occur in our own churches? We have already talked about the approach that some people use—they leave or drop out. Leaving for another church is an unhealthy approach because we will just find different conflicts in the new church. Dropping out altogether is unhealthy because it deprives us of the spiritual nurturing that we need as Christians. It is also an avoidance behavior that does not work in the long run because we will still be facing conflicts in other areas of our life. How can we find an approach to conflict in the church that also helps us deal with conflict in other venues?

Looking at the example of Acts, we need to first of all encourage the listening and sharing process. The leaders of the Grecian community were straightforward enough to share their concern, and the Twelve and others were caring enough to listen to them. Then a solution was arrived at that included giving responsibility and power to the disaffected part of the community. This was not a situation where one faction overpowered the other, but rather a situation that was "win-win." Here are some actions that can help us toward this same kind of "win-win" solution:

1. VISIT WITH THE PASTOR AND SEVERAL LAY PEOPLE TO FIND OUT WHO ARE THE DISAFFECTED GROUPS IN YOUR CHURCH. Take some time to listen to representatives of these groups. Listening to them doesn't mean that you have to agree with them, but do be careful to not listen defensively, or else the sharing process will be short-lived. Share the insights you have from doing this with your pastor or lay leaders.

2. COMPARE THE MAKEUP OF THE GOVERNING BOARD OR BODY OF YOUR CHURCH WITH THE MAKEUP OF THE CONGREGATION AS A WHOLE. Are some groups in the church under- or over-represented on the governing body? Discuss with your pastor and/or nominating committee what it might mean to rectify this inequity. Are there even new types of leadership positions that can be created (as in our passage for today) that might help disaffected members feel more a part of what is happening in your church?

Why should you pray for those who have a different perspective than you?

3. PRAY FOR PEOPLE IN YOUR CHURCH WHO HAVE A DIFFERENT PERSPECTIVE OR NEED THAN YOU AND THE GROUPS OF WHICH YOU FEEL A PART. This can remind you of your oneness in the Spirit and help you to see the world as they see it.

CARING TIME
Remain in groups of 6–8 people, in a horseshoe configuration.

Hand out the Prayer/ Praise Report to the entire group. Ask each subgroup to pray for the empty chair. Pray specifically for God to guide you to someone to bring next week to fill that chair.

After a sufficient time of prayer in subgroups, close in a corporate prayer. Say, "Next week we will talk about: 'A Dramatic Conversion.'"

Remind participants of the daily Scripture readings and reflective questions found on page 41.

Caring Time (15-20 minutes)

Close by taking time to pray for one another and for your own special concerns. Begin by having each group member finish the sentence:

"The greatest challenge or conflict I see facing me in the weeks ahead will be ..."

Then pray for God's strength and direction in the midst of these challenges. Also, use the Prayer/Praise Report and pray for the requests and concerns listed.

notes:

BIBLE STUDY NOTES

Reference Notes

Use these notes to gain further understanding of the text as you study on your own:

ACTS 6:1
widows

Many elderly Jews who had lived most of their lives elsewhere in the empire came to live in Jerusalem for their final years. Those who were widowed, now far from home, were subject to poverty. It was these women who were being neglected.

Grecian Jews. These were Jews who came from outside Palestine and for whom Aramaic and Hebrew were relatively unknown languages. Their synagogue worship was also conducted in their native languages.

Hebraic Jews. These were native to the land who spoke Aramaic as their daily language. Since all the apostles were Hebraic Jews, it may be that they were naturally more sensitive and aware of the needs of those with whom they could easily communicate.

ACTS 6:2
deacons

wait on tables. Literally, "to serve tables." This does not refer to being a waiter. Since banking at the time was done by people sitting at a table, to "serve tables" was a figure of speech for handling financial transactions. While many groups use this passage as the basis for the office of deacon, there is no title given to these men. However, the Greek verb "to serve" is the root word from which the English word "deacon" comes.

ACTS 6:5
chosen to serve

The names of the men chosen strongly indicate that all seven were Greek-speaking Jews. They perhaps also served as a bridge between the apostles and the Greek-speaking Jews to help avoid further unintentional difficulties between the two groups.

Stephen. This man moves to center stage in chapter 7, where he becomes the first Christian martyr.

Philip. Like Stephen, Philip demonstrated gifts of evangelism not unlike those of the apostles (v. 8; 8:4-8; 21:8). Of the other men nothing more is known.

ACTS 6:6
blessing

laid their hands on them. In the Old Testament the laying on of hands signified either a blessing (Gen. 48:14) or a commissioning (Num. 27:18,23).

ACTS 6:7
devout men

priests. While the Sadducees controlled the priesthood, many of the priests, like Zechariah the father of John the Baptist (Luke 1:5-6), were sincerely devout men.

notes:

Session

5

A Dramatic Conversion

Prepare for the Session

	READINGS	REFLECTIVE QUESTIONS
Monday	Acts 9:1–6	What answers are you seeking of Jesus today? What is He asking of you?
Tuesday	Acts 9:7–9	In what ways are you "blind" right now? To what is God seeking to open your eyes?
Wednesday	Acts 9:10–15	How are you letting fear come between you and others who are brothers and sisters in Christ?
Thursday	Acts 9:32–35	In what ways are you suffering from "paralysis"—not acting when you are needing to act? What needs to happen in order for you to be "healed"?
Friday	Acts 9:36–39	Were you to die, what would your family and friends remember most about you?
Saturday	Acts 9:40	What is dead inside of you that needs to be brought to life? How could faith help make you well?
Sunday	Acts 9:41	Whom do you need to "help to their feet" right now?

notes:

OUR GOALS FOR THIS SESSION ARE:

In groups of 6–8, gather people in a horseshoe configuration.

Make sure everyone has a name tag.

Take time to share information on class parties that are coming up as well as any relevant church events.

INTRODUCE THE ICEBREAKER ACTIVITY: The students have been told in their books to choose one answer.

After the Icebreaker say something like, "The Apostle Paul also came to a fork in the road of his life. As Saul he had been a persecutor of the church, but Christ called him in a new direction. In today's session we will look at what that meant to Paul, and what it means for the changes we are called to make in our own lives."

Hand out the Prayer/Praise Report. A sample copy is on pages 158-159. Have people write down prayer requests and praises. Then have the prayer coordinator collect the report and make copies for use during the Caring Time.

BIBLE STUDY

- to consider what happened when Jesus came and turned Saul's life around
- to get a better understanding of what happens in dramatic conversions like Saul's
- to take a look at the need for support from others after conversion

LIFE CHANGE

- to share our faith with at least one person we have previously seen as a "threat"
- to "adopt" a new Christian in our church (either as a class or as an individual)
- to encourage the starting of a Christian recovery group

Icebreaker (10-15 minutes)

Forks in the Road. An oft-repeated Yogi Berra saying is, "When you come to a fork in the road—take it." Well, we all come to forks in the road of our life, and *probably* what Yogi Berra was trying to say is that when that happens we have to make a decision and go one way or the other. Use the following questions to share your reaction to forks in the road, both real and hypothetical. Go around the group on question 1 and let everyone share. Then go around again on question 2.

1. If you came to a fork in the road between the following options, which path would you take?

being a famous entertainer	being a CEO of a big corporation
spending a summer in Europe	spending a summer landscaping my yard
traveling to Mars	retreating to a castle in Spain
spending a year exploring an archaeological site	spending a year exploring America's great shopping malls

notes:

Icebreaker (cont'd)

2. Which of the following "forks in the road" did you have the hardest time "taking"?

the life of a "carefree" single	the life of a family person
small town life	big city life
following my dreams	following a practical career
doing it "my way"	doing it the Lord's way

LEARNING FROM THE BIBLE

ACTS 9:1-19

Have four members of the class, selected ahead of time, read the passage from Acts. Have one member read the narration, one member read the part of Jesus (vv. 4b, 5b-6, 10b, 11-12, 15-16), one member read the part of Saul (v. 5), and one member read the part of Ananias (vv. 10c, 13-14, 17b).

Bible Study (30-45 minutes)

The Scripture for this week:

*1Meanwhile, Saul was still breathing out murderous threats
against the Lord's disciples. He went to the high priest 2and asked
him for letters to the synagogues in Damascus, so that if he found
any there who belonged to the Way, whether men or women, he
might take them as prisoners to Jerusalem. 3As he neared Damascus
on his journey, suddenly a light from heaven flashed around him.
4He fell to the ground and heard a voice say to him, "Saul, Saul, why
do you persecute me?"*

5"Who are you, Lord?" Saul asked.

*"I am Jesus, whom you are persecuting," he replied. 6"Now get
up and go into the city, and you will be told what you must do."*

*7"The men traveling with Saul stood there speechless; they heard
the sound but did not see anyone. 8Saul got up from the ground, but
when he opened his eyes he could see nothing. So they led him by the
hand into Damascus. 9For three days he was blind, and did not eat
or drink anything.*

*10In Damascus there was a disciple named Ananias. The Lord
called to him in a vision, "Ananias!"*

"Yes, Lord," he answered.

*11The Lord told him, "Go to the house of Judas on Straight Street
and ask for a man from Tarsus named Saul, for he is praying. 12In a
vision he has seen a man named Ananias come and place his hands
on him to restore his sight."*

[13]"Lord," Ananias answered, "I have heard many reports about this man and all the harm he has done to your saints in Jerusalem. [14]And he has come here with authority from the chief priests to arrest all who call on your name."

[15]But the Lord said to Ananias, "Go! This man is my chosen instrument to carry my name before the Gentiles and their kings and before the people of Israel. [16]I will show him how much he must suffer for my name."

[17]Then Ananias went to the house and entered it. Placing his hands on Saul, he said, "Brother Saul, the Lord—Jesus, who appeared to you on the road as you were coming here—has sent me so that you may see again and be filled with the Holy Spirit." [18]Immediately, something like scales fell from Saul's eyes, and he could see again. He got up and was baptized, [19]and after taking some food, he regained his strength.

notes:

Summarize these introductory remarks. Be sure to include the underlined information, which gives the answers to the student book questions (provided in the margin).

What factors do some people say predetermine a person's life?

...about today's session (5 minutes)

A NEW PERSPECTIVE

Some people have the philosophy, "The more people change, the more they stay the same." Some will even say that a person's life is determined by a combination of their genes and their experiences in the first three or four years of life. If a person buys into this perspective then they may start believing that there is no hope for someone who is trapped by destructive behavior. Alcoholics will forever be losing their battle to alcohol. People with an eating problem will never conquer it and will forever be overweight. And people who are your enemy will always be your enemy. The New Testament testifies to the falseness of this perspective. Its pages recount a collage of lives changed by the power of Jesus Christ. Nowhere is this seen more clearly than in the story of Saul's (Paul's) conversion. He went from being a vehement opponent and persecutor of Christianity to being its strongest, most influential adherent.

...about today's session (cont'd)

In what ways can Saul's conversion be important to us personally?

The conversion of the persecutor known as Saul to the missionary known as Paul was not the minor reform of a backsliding individual. It was a dramatic, permanent change in life direction. This story not only has historical significance, but it can also have personal significance as we seek to change our own lives. That Saul made this turn-around means we can too. By studying his story we can perhaps discover within it the elements that are part of real life change. That is what we will be seeking to do in this session.

notes:

Remain in groups of 6–8 people, in a horseshoe configuration.

In this small-group session, students will be responding to the following questions that will help them share their stories in terms of Paul's dramatic conversion.

Have the students explore these questions together.

Identifying with the Story (5-7 minutes)

1. Who were you most likely to "persecute" when you were in grade school or junior high?

- ☐ nerds
- ☐ a younger brother or sister
- ☐ an older brother or sister
- ☐ the fat kids
- ☐ the opposite sex
- ☐ kids of another culture
- ☐ my parents
- ☐ other:______________

2. If Christ were to meet you on the road and call you on the carpet for something you used to do in your younger years, what would it be?

3. In your own coming to Christ, who was the Ananias whom God used to help turn you around?

Share with your class the following information which you may modify according to your own perspectives and teaching needs. The answers to the student book questions (provided in the margin) are underlined.

today's session (15-20 minutes)

One thing the Bible doesn't seem to do is look at its central characters through rose-colored glasses and try to make them out to be overly perfect heroes. Moses murdered a man. David had an affair with Bathsheba, and tried to cover it up by a murder. Peter denied his Lord. And now in Acts we read the story of Saul, who later became Paul, the Christian church's greatest evangelist. When we first hear of him, he is a persecutor of the church, cooperating with a lynch mob (Acts 7:54–8:1). And now, in this passage, he is taking a more active role in seeking to imprison and even kill Christians. That the Bible is so honest about its heroes should help us to trust it even more.

What effect should it have upon us that the Bible is so honest about its heroes?

Saul's Persecution of the Church

Let's look more closely at this story. Saul asks for "letters to the synagogues in Damascus" (v. 2). Such official letters were the means of granting legitimacy to a courier whom the Jews at Damascus would not have otherwise known. According to 1 Maccabees 15:15 the Romans had granted to the high priest the right of extraditing to Jerusalem Jewish troublemakers who had fled abroad. This would cover the case of Christians from Jerusalem who had taken refuge in Damascus. And so Saul went to Damascus looking for those belonging to "the Way." (It was not until later at Antioch that they were first called "Christians.") In any case, even then they were seen not as a distinctly new religion, but as a group within Judaism. He went in order to bring them back to be tried by the Sanhedrin. It was a kind of first-century inquisition. However, this inquisition was short-circuited by Saul's own life change.

What name was given to Christianity at this time?

5

How Saul Changed

Saul's vision on the road to Damascus is one of the most profound conversion stories in history. As Paul, he later referred to it no less than four times to validate his authority as an apostle (1 Cor. 9:1; 15:8; 2 Cor. 4:6; Gal. 1:15-16). Saul later equated his vision of the risen Lord with those who saw Jesus in the flesh before His death and resurrection. Such a direct, face-to-face experience with Jesus was needed to have the status of an apostle. It is significant then that the others who traveled with Saul "heard the sound but did not see anyone" (v. 7).

Saul's encounter with Christ changed his life forever. His life change was not simply a matter of personal resolve, such as we might try to muster with a New Year's resolution. It was his relationship with his new Lord and Master that gave him the power to change.

What gave Saul the power to change?

today's session (cont'd)

What were some aspects of Saul's personality that may not have changed?

Certainly there were aspects of Saul's personality that did not change. The zeal he showed in persecuting Christians (Gal. 1:14) became zeal in preaching the gospel. Similarly, the emotional volatility he evidences in his letters (2 Cor. 11:1-21; Gal. 1:8-9) and in Acts (23:2-5) was probably a lifelong pattern. The point is not that people change in entirety, but that they can change their essential life direction. This is the ability that Paul showed through the grace of Jesus Christ.

What evidence is there that Saul, later called Paul, may have had continuing vision problems?

After his vision of Jesus, we are told that Saul's eyes were open but he could see nothing. God used Ananias to perform the miracle that restored Saul's sight. However, there are indications that Saul (Paul) may have had continued problems with his sight. He had someone else pen his letters (Rom 16:22), and when he did write with his own hand he noted how big the letters were (Gal. 6:11).

The Role of Ananias

The role Ananias played in Saul's conversion should not be shortchanged. He knew what Saul had done and was planning to do to the Christians in Damascus. Like most of us would be in similar circumstances, he was worried for his own safety. Yet, because God called him to witness, he put his own fears aside and obeyed God. What would have happened had he not done so? It's easy to say that God would have found another way to restore Saul's sight and get him started on his ministry, and certainly He could have. But we do know that Ananias' role was pivotal. This reminds us that human change is not a "pull yourself up by your own bootstraps" phenomenon. Human change most often requires a supportive friendship or community. Recovery programs like AA have recognized this for some time, providing supportive meetings and a sponsor to help the person through their transition. Ananias was like Paul's "sponsor" in his life change.

In what way might Ananias have been an example to Paul in ministerial style?

Ananias also modeled a good ministerial style for Paul. Some people take on what might be called a "defensive" style of ministry. That is, the main role they see themselves taking is defending themselves and other Christians against the "threats" they see in others around them, particularly non-Christians. There certainly are such threats in our time, as there were in the time of Acts. However, the approach God called Ananias to take was an "offensive" style of ministry. Instead of focusing on defending against the "threat" of Saul, he was encouraged to go on the offensive and witness to Saul in the name of Christ. This was an example that Saul, as Paul the missionary, later probably drew upon as he faced many different kinds of people, many of whom he could have viewed as threats. But Paul saw people as potential converts rather than as threats. (See, for example, Acts 26:24-29.)

In order to heal Saul, Ananias laid his hands on him. Laying on of hands was a common way of conveying the Holy Spirit (Acts 8:17-18; 13:3; 19:6). It was the Spirit that in turn healed Paul of his blindness. Certainly this physical blindness was symbolic of the spiritual blindness that Saul had evidenced in persecuting the church. He was cured of both forms of blindness by the Holy Spirit.

Paul's Witness

Paul's witness after this event was particularly powerful due to the radical change in his life. It was so powerful that the Jewish traditionalists wasted no time in trying to kill him. (The text in verse 23 says "the Jews," but remember Paul and many other Christians were Jews as well. In Acts, the term "the Jews" refers to the traditional Jewish leadership.) In a similar way, Jewish religious leadership in Jerusalem sought to kill Lazarus after he had been raised from the dead, so powerful was his testimony (John 12:10). To save Saul, the other disciples of Damascus had to go out at night to lower him in a basket through an opening in the wall (Acts 9:25). It would not be the last time that Saul would be in danger because of his boldness in proclaiming the gospel of Christ. His life change had taken him from being the hunter to being the hunted. But it was a life change that he would have said made it all worth it!

notes:

Remain in groups of 6–8 people, in a horseshoe configuration.

In this small-group session, students will be applying the lessons of the text to their own lives through the following questions.

The students were asked (in the student book) to choose an answer for each question and explain why.

Learning from the Story (5-7 minutes)

1. What do you believe motivated Saul in his zeal for persecuting Christians?

- ☐ a sincere desire to do what was right
- ☐ a desire to win political points with the high priest
- ☐ a need to quiet his own doubts by attacking divergent opinions
- ☐ a desire to win points with God
- ☐ other: ____________________

2. When Saul saw his vision on the road to Damascus, it was:

- ☐ an hallucination
- ☐ the result of a buildup of guilt
- ☐ an intervention of God
- ☐ a moment of intuitive insight

3. Had you been Ananias, and God called on you to go minister to Saul, how would you have responded?

- ☐ "Here am I, send ... him!"
- ☐ "I don't do charity cases."
- ☐ "Surely, Lord, you jest!"
- ☐ "And who will watch my back?"
- ☐ "If you say so, Lord."

notes:

Share with the class the following thoughts on how the lessons of this text might be applied today. The answers to the student book questions (provided in the margin) are underlined unless the question requires a personal answer.

What does a church that wants to model itself on the church of Acts need to believe?

Why is it important that we also believe in God's power to change us?

life change lessons (5-7 minutes)

Life change happens when Christians believe in God's power to change lives. Therefore a church that wants to model itself on the church of Acts needs to believe in that awesome power. We need to believe in God's power both to change us and to change the people to whom we seek to witness. We need to believe in God's power to continue to change us, even though we have already made our commitment to Jesus Christ. Unless we are living, changing people, nobody is going to want to listen to our witness and have what we have. Bob Dylan once said, "He who isn't busy being born is busy dying." No one wants to be part of a church of stagnating, dying people.

We also need to believe in God's power to change those people to whom we seek to witness. We need to believe in God's power to change the alcoholic as well as the CEO addicted to power. We need to believe in God's power to change the prostitute as well as the mid-level executive who has sold out his or her principles "for the good of the company." We need to believe in God's power to change the man or woman involved in domestic abuse as well as the computer hacker who abuses his or her knowledge by sending out computer viruses.

Believing in God's power to change people also means being the kind of church through whom God can change people. In order to be that kind of body, here are some suggestions for action based on what we have learned:

1. SHARE YOUR FAITH WITH AT LEAST ONE PERSON YOU HAVE PREVIOUSLY SEEN AS A THREAT. This can be someone of another culture or lifestyle (a young person with spiked green hair and tattoos) or someone who is your rival at work. Be careful to share from the perspective of an equal and fellow struggler, and not from someone who has already arrived spiritually.

2. EITHER AS A CLASS OR AS AN INDIVIDUAL, "ADOPT" A NEW CHRISTIAN IN YOUR CHURCH. This can mean inviting the person to class functions, calling them up to see how things are going in their spiritual growth, introducing them to other people in the church, or in other ways encouraging them. You can be this person's "Ananias."

3. ENCOURAGE THE STARTING OF A CHRISTIAN RECOVERY GROUP. There are groups that deal with everything from alcohol and drugs to overeating to sexual addiction. Many of these groups just need meeting space in order to carry out their ministry. Your hospitality should include the understanding that members are invited to come and be part of your other worship, fellowship, and educational activities.

CARING TIME
Remain in groups of 6–8 people, in a horseshoe configuration.

Hand out the Prayer/Praise Report to the entire group. Ask each subgroup to pray for the empty chair. Pray specifically for God to guide you to someone to bring next week to fill that chair.

After a sufficient time of prayer in subgroups, close in a corporate prayer. Say, "Next week we will talk about: 'The Community Expands.'"

Remind participants of the daily Scripture readings and reflective questions found on page 51.

Caring Time (15-20 minutes)

Remember that this time is to develop and express your care for each other by sharing personal prayer requests and praying for each other's needs. Begin by having each group member finish the sentence:

"Right now I need an Ananias to help me ..."

Then pray for God's strength to make these changes and to be an "Ananias" for each other. Also, use the Prayer/Praise Report and pray for the concerns listed.

notes:

BIBLE STUDY NOTES

Reference Notes

Use these notes to gain further understanding of the text as you study on your own:

ACTS 9:1
Saul's persecution

breathing out murderous threats. This reflects the depth of Saul's obsessive hatred toward the Christians. After hearing Stephen's speech (7:1-53), he undoubtedly viewed the Christians as an antiestablishment, heretical sect determined to undermine the Law of God and the worship of the temple. His ability to carry out his threats of murder would certainly have been proscribed by Roman law, but apparently he and the Sanhedrin had some success in their program (26:10).

ACTS 9:2
the Way

letters. While the Sanhedrin had no formal authority outside of Judea, its prestige could influence elders in synagogues far from Jerusalem. In this case, the Sanhedrin asked the elders in Damascus to cooperate with Saul by allowing him to arrest as blasphemers those Christians who had fled from Jerusalem to Damascus and bring them for trial in Jerusalem. The Book of Maccabees speaks of the Sanhedrin requesting officials in Egypt to give them extradition rights over Palestinian law-breakers who had fled there.
Damascus. A city about 150 miles from Jerusalem. Luke has not told us how the church began among the sizable Jewish community in this important city, but Saul desired to expand his persecution there so that it might not spread any further. This incident reveals how central Saul was to the

ACTS 9:2
the Way
(cont'd)

carrying out of this first wave of persecution: once he was converted, this persecution dissipated (9:31).
the Way. This phrase is unique to Acts as a name for Christianity (19:9,23; 22:4; 24:14,22). It may stem from Jesus' claim in John 14:6.

ACTS 9:3
glory

a light from heaven flashed around him. The term is often used of lightning, indicating the brilliance of the light (Acts 26:13). Light (glory) is commonly connected with divine appearances (Luke 9:29; Rev. 1:14-16).

ACTS 9:4
the body of Christ

why do you persecute me. The opposition Saul created for the church was really directed against its Head, Jesus, demonstrating the identity between Jesus and the church, His body (Luke 10:16). God is bringing Saul face-to-face with the fact that by his activities he is not honoring God, but resisting the One glorified by God.

ACTS 9:9

This profound experience shattered all of Saul's previous convictions. Humbled and blinded, he fasted as he awaited what Jesus would do next with him.

ACTS 9:10

Apart from Paul's comment in Acts 22:12, nothing is known of Ananias.

ACTS 9:11–12
vision

The vision Ananias received was matched by one Saul had of his coming. This double-dream confirmation is also seen in the story of Peter and Cornelius (ch. 10).
Straight Street. The street that is called Straight, where Saul's host lived, is still one of the main thoroughfares of Damascus. The house of Judas is traditionally located near its western end. Nothing is known of Judas.

5

ACTS 9:13–14
holy ones

Lord. This title for Jesus, highlighting His authority, is a common one in this account (vv. 5,11,13,15,17), and in Paul's writings.
saints. Literally, "holy ones." This was a common term for Israel in the Old Testament. Ananias applies it to Christians, as does Paul in his letters. It means those people who are separated out for God.
all who call on your name. This way of referring to Christians comes from Joel 2:32. In the Book of Joel it was God's name (Yahweh) that was to be called upon: the fact that the early Christians transferred this to Jesus is a clear indication of their belief in His divinity.

ACTS 9:15–16
a light to the Gentiles

The Lord overruled Ananias with a final command to "Go!" and a description of what Saul's mission would be.
my chosen instrument. Literally, "a choice vessel." Some images from the Old Testament form the context here. Israel was compared to a vessel in the hand of a potter, formed to perform the task for which the potter created it (Jer. 18:1-6). The Servant of Isaiah was God's chosen (Isa. 44:1): Saul (soon to be Paul) would carry on the mission of the Servant in terms of bringing the light to the Gentiles (Isa. 42:6; 49:6) and in sharing in his suffering.

ACTS 9:17–19
sight restored

Brother Saul. Without further question, Ananias affirms Saul as part of the family through the grace of Jesus. After laying hands on him, Saul's sight was restored; he was baptized (presumably by Ananias); and was filled with the Holy Spirit.

Session 6

The Community Expands

Prepare for the Session

	READINGS	REFLECTIVE QUESTIONS
Monday	Acts 10:1-8	What might an angel of God say about your prayer life right now?
Tuesday	Acts 10:9-16	When has God showed you a new perspective on your beliefs? How did you respond?
Wednesday	Acts 10:17-23	How would your outreach to others be different if you truly believed that no person or group of persons was "unclean"?
Thursday	Acts 11:19-21	In what ways might God be calling you to go beyond your "comfort zone"?
Friday	Acts 11:22-24	Who has encouraged you lately? How can you encourage someone this week?
Saturday	Acts 11:25-26	Who has especially helped you in the work you do? How can you thank this person?
Sunday	Acts 11:27-30	In what area of your life are you experiencing a "famine"? How could your Christian brothers and sisters help you in the midst of this "famine"?

notes:

OUR GOALS FOR THIS SESSION ARE:

In groups of 6–8, gather people in a horseshoe configuration.

Make sure everyone has a name tag.

Take time to share information on class parties that are coming up as well as any relevant church events.

INTRODUCE THE ICEBREAKER ACTIVITY: The students have been told in their books to choose one answer.

After the Icebreaker say something like, "Just like 'uninvited' persons have come into our lives, so the community of the early church expanded when God invited some people who had previously been uninvited—Gentiles. When that happened, the church really caught fire. In this session, we will be talking about how the same thing can happen today."

Hand out the Prayer/Praise Report. A sample copy is on pages 158-159. Have people write down prayer requests and praises. Then have the prayer coordinator collect the report and make copies for use during the Caring Time.

BIBLE STUDY
- to see how the Christian community of Acts expanded to include Gentiles
- to understand what it means for us today that we should not call anyone "impure or unclean"
- to acknowledge how the Christian community is strengthened by being multicultural

LIFE CHANGE
- to discover what cultural groups are present in the community, but are under-represented in the churches
- to invite someone from another culture into our homes
- to initiate a pulpit exchange, combined worship, or social function between our church and an ethnic church

Icebreaker (10-15 minutes)

Uninvited. In the following questions, share the role "uninvited" persons have played in your life. Go around the group on question 1 and let everyone share. Then go around again on question 2.

1. What person or persons would you have seen as "uninvited" in your life when you were in high school?
   - ☐ nerds
   - ☐ Christian kids who kept trying to convert me
   - ☐ the druggies
   - ☐ a prodigal parent who didn't live with us
   - ☐ kids of other racial groups
   - ☐ adults in general
   - ☐ other: ______________________

2. When has someone you considered to be "uninvited" broken through and become a significant part of your life?

notes:

6

LEARNING FROM THE BIBLE

ACTS 10:1-23

Have six members of the class, selected ahead of time, read the passage from Acts. One member should read the narrative portion. Another should read the part of the angel/ voice (vv. 3c, 4b–6,13, 15,19b-20); the third should read the part of Cornelius (v. 4a); the fourth the part of Peter (vv. 14,21) and the fifth and sixth the part of the men (v. 22).

Bible Study (30-45 minutes)

The Scripture for this week:

[1]At Caesarea there was a man named Cornelius, a centurion in what was known as the Italian Regiment. [2]He and all his family were devout and God-fearing; he gave generously to those in need and prayed to God regularly. [3]One day at about three in the afternoon he had a vision. He distinctly saw an angel of God, who came to him and said, "Cornelius!"

[4]Cornelius stared at him in fear. "What is it, Lord?" he asked.

The angel answered, "Your prayers and gifts to the poor have come up as a memorial offering before God. [5]Now send men to Joppa to bring back a man named Simon who is called Peter. [6]He is staying with Simon the tanner, whose house is by the sea."

[7]When the angel who spoke to him had gone, Cornelius called two of his servants and a devout soldier who was one of his attendants. [8]He told them everything that had happened and sent them to Joppa.

[9]About noon the following day as they were on their journey and approaching the city, Peter went up on the roof to pray. [10]He became hungry and wanted something to eat, and while the meal was being prepared, he fell into a trance. [11]He saw heaven opened and something like a large sheet being let down to earth by its four corners. [12]It contained all kinds of four-footed animals, as well as reptiles of the earth and birds of the air. [13]Then a voice told him, "Get up, Peter. Kill and eat."

[14]"Surely not, Lord!" Peter replied. "I have never eaten anything impure or unclean."

[15]The voice spoke to him a second time, "Do not call anything impure that God has made clean."

[16]This happened three times, and immediately the sheet was taken back to heaven.

[17]While Peter was wondering about the meaning of the vision, the men sent by Cornelius found out where Simon's house was and stopped at the gate. [18]They called out, asking if Simon who was known as Peter was staying there.

[19]While Peter was still thinking about the vision, the Spirit said to him, "Simon, three men are looking for you. [20]So get up and go downstairs. Do not hesitate to go with them, for I have sent them."

[21]Peter went down and said to the men, "I'm the one you're looking for. Why have you come?"

22The men replied, "We have come from Cornelius the centurion.
He is a righteous and God-fearing man, who is respected by all the
Jewish people. A holy angel told him to have you come to his house
so that he could hear what you have to say." 23Then Peter invited the
men into the house to be his guests.

notes:

Summarize these introductory remarks. Be sure to include the underlined information, which gives the answers to the student book questions (provided in the margin).

What situations could one point to in support of the idea that we really can't "all get along"?

What is the key to turning former enemies into friends?

...about today's session (5 minutes)

GETTING ALONG

A few years ago, after a well-publicized incident of law enforcement impropriety, Rodney King asked the oft-quoted question, "Why can't we all just get along?" Looking around us we see plenty of situations that seem to cry out for an answer to that question. African-Americans and Hispanics continue to be victims of racial profiling; hate groups spread their venom over the Internet; and armed hostilities in Ireland and the Middle East create tension between supporters of opposing sides in our own country. If we look at our morning paper, our answer would have to be that we just can't get along.

If we look at how Christ has changed people and how the church has brought together former enemies, however, we get a much different answer to Rodney King's question: we can get along if we submit ourselves to Jesus Christ and take seriously His teachings. Now we don't want to try to claim too much here. It is true that people in the church don't always get along with each other, and that sometimes Christians have even gone to war with those of other faiths, such as in the Crusades. The key is the second part of what we said: we must *take seriously* Christ's teachings. It's not a matter of "make everyone believe what Christians believe and we will all get along;" but rather, "If Christians truly live out Christ's teachings on loving one another, not judging others, and valuing each person as a creature of God, then we will be amazed at what former enemies can be our friends."

In the Scripture passage for today we find two people who had formerly been enemies becoming brothers in Christ. As we look at this story, we will gain new insights on how this can happen today as well.

Remain in groups of 6–8 people, in a horseshoe configuration.

In this small-group session, students will be responding to the following questions that will help them share their stories in terms of Peter's vision and Cornelius.

Have the students explore these questions together.

Identifying with the Story (5-7 minutes)

1. If this were your vision, what kind of food would come down in the sheet?

- ☐ meat of any kind—I'm a vegetarian.
- ☐ raw oysters
- ☐ deer or game meat
- ☐ liver
- ☐ cow's tongue or brains
- ☐ anything with artificial preservatives
- ☐ tofu or other "health food"
- ☐ the same things that were in Peter's sheet—I don't do reptiles!
- ☐ Nothing would be in it, because I'll eat anything!

2. When have you, like Peter, had a dream through which you suspected God might be trying to tell you something?

3. Which people or groups would God have to first open your heart to in a vision or dream before you would socialize with and witness to them?

- ☐ homeless people
- ☐ homosexuals
- ☐ alcoholics or drug addicts
- ☐ KKK or hate group members
- ☐ sexual offenders
- ☐ people of another race or culture
- ☐ youth with spiked dog collars and tattoos
- ☐ prostitutes
- ☐ ex-convicts
- ☐ the wealthy country club set
- ☐ other: ______________________

notes:

today's session (15-20 minutes)

Share with your class the following information which you may modify according to your own perspectives and teaching needs. The answers to the student book questions (provided in the margin) are underlined.

What was perhaps the biggest cultural division of biblical times?

Perhaps the biggest cultural division of biblical times was the division between Jews and Gentiles. It would have been comparable to the division between blacks and Caucasians, Arabs and Jews, or Japanese and Koreans in our modern society. To understand what God did to heal this division in the church, we first need to understand how it came about.

The Origin of Separateness

Why did God originally want the people of Israel to separate themselves from the people around them?

God had called the Jews to be distinct from the people around them, and this included what they could and couldn't eat. Peter was a good Jew and followed Old Testament dietary laws (Lev. 11:1-47). The importance of many of these laws may seem to elude us today, but they were probably grounded in health issues. They were also part of what separated Jews from the people around them. Such a separation needed to happen so that Jews wouldn't just blend into other cultures, all of which worshiped other gods, and some of which practiced the especially abominable practices of child sacrifice and cult prostitution. God wanted them to see themselves as different than the people who did such practices. However, there is sometimes a fine line between hating the behavior of a people and hating the people, and over time many Jews came to hate all Gentiles.

It was in this context that the story about Peter occurs. It helps us to understand that when this event happened in the life of Peter, God wasn't just changing a dietary law. Rather, He was announcing a change in the way Jews were to look at the people of the cultures around them. Let's look at the specific things that are said in this story.

The Gospel Comes to Cornelius

Why would Cornelius have been especially hated?

In verse 1, we learn that Cornelius was "a centurion." As such he was a representative of the military oppression of Rome, a hated foreign culture. We read in verse 2 that he was "God-fearing." This was a phrase that generally meant he was not a full proselyte to Judaism, but he believed in the God of Judaism. Such a person believed, but may have avoided becoming a convert because of being put off by Jewish ceremonial law. In verse 2, we also read that Cornelius "gave generously to those in need" and "prayed to God regularly." Thus he loved God and neighbor, as the two greatest commandments called him to do.

Cornelius is instructed to send for Peter. But why Peter? Paul had yet to begin his Gentile mission, and he had recently been converted. Since he had much learning and preparation to do, Paul would not have been a candidate at this point in time. Still, the choice of Peter seems a little strange at first. Peter, even after this vision, had his hesitancy about accepting Gentiles outright (Gal. 2:11-13). But perhaps God was sending Cornelius to the church leader who most needed a change of heart about Gentiles. If you have feelings of hostility toward a group, it makes a difference if you really get to know someone who is part of the group you have opposed or disliked. A good movie on how this works between races is "Remember the Titans" with Denzel Washington. In this film, high school football players from a formerly all-black school and high school football players from a formerly all-white school, learn to play together as one, and to love each other as brothers. That is how the church should be.

Why does it seem a little strange that Cornelius was instructed to send for Peter? How did God use this situation to teach Peter?

No Impure People in Christ

In verse 9 we read, "Peter went up on the roof to pray." This was not unusual because roofs were flat and often served the same function as a porch or deck might today—a place to sit and reflect or socialize with others. That he went there to pray meant that he was open to a message from God. When we go to talk to God, we should always be mindful that maybe God has something to say to us. Verse 9 also tells us that Peter went to pray at "about noon." Many devout Jews prayed regularly at 9 a.m., noon, and 3 p.m. In verse 12, we find that Peter saw "all kinds" of creatures, reptiles, and birds being lowered to the ground on "something like a large sheet." These animals included those that the Law had proscribed as food. A voice from heaven called to Peter for him to kill these animals and eat them! For him it would have been about the same as a voice from heaven telling us to go out and commit murder. Many persons would have a tendency to doubt it was from God.

At what times did devout Jews generally pray?

Why did Peter hesitate to follow the directions of the voice in his vision?

When Peter hesitated to follow the instruction of the voice, he was told, "Do not call anything impure that God has made clean" (v. 15). The voice convinced Peter and he had a new insight about human relationships. When he later went to Cornelius, he shared what he had learned, "God has shown me that I should not call any man impure or unclean" (v. 28).

What is the central concept that Peter learned from his vision?

The challenge for us, as it was for Israel, is how to separate ourselves from impure behavior without judging and separating ourselves from people. We have been taught not to abuse our bodies with drugs and alcohol. But we cannot treat addicts as if they are spiritually unworthy and impure. We have been taught to be sexually responsible. But we cannot treat prostitutes or the sexually addicted as if they are spiritually unworthy or impure. And, of course, it is especially tragic and sinful when we reject persons as "impure" simply because of their race, while their faith and behavior could even be exemplary. What we do need to do, then, is to love each one as a brother or sister in Christ. We need to acknowledge that each one is loved and precious to God.

If what God is teaching us in this passage is true, why don't we take it more seriously in how the church functions? The statement has been made that "Eleven O'Clock Sunday morning is the most segregated hour in America." Yet the church must lead by example! The people of the world will never start getting along unless the church takes seriously the direction of their Savior and Lord, and starts showing the way by loving and accepting each other across cultures and other divisions.

notes:

6

Remain in groups of 6–8 people, in a horseshoe configuration.

In this small-group session, students will be applying the lessons of the text to their own lives through the following questions.

The students were asked (in the student book) to choose an answer for each question and explain why.

Learning from the Story (5-7 minutes)

1. What impresses you most about Cornelius?
   - ☐ Though raised in a polytheistic culture, he was committed to the one true God.
   - ☐ Though a military man in an occupying force, he cared for the people.
   - ☐ He was generous to the poor.
   - ☐ He was obedient to the vision given to him.

2. Had you been Peter, what would have been going through your mind when you saw the vision of the animals in the sheet?
   - ☐ "Is this some kind of trick of the Devil?"
   - ☐ "Is God changing the rules in the middle of the game?"
   - ☐ "I think I might not be so hungry after all!"
   - ☐ "What is God trying to tell me?" ________________

3. How would it change your behavior if you believed in your heart that all people were "clean"?

life change lessons (5-7 minutes)

Share with the class the following thoughts on how the lessons of this text might be applied today. The answers to the student book questions (provided in the margin) are underlined unless the question requires a personal answer.

If every church leader could have a vision from God that expanded his or her view of whom their church needed to reach out to, our churches would all be exploding with new ministries and new members. Unfortunately, not every church leader seems to be granted such a vision. Perhaps God knows not every church leader would respond with the openness and obedience that Peter showed. In any case, what can we do to best expand our vision of how to include others in our Christian communities? Some churches only seem to be concerned with drawing more people "like themselves." In certain situations, it might even work for a while to reach out only to those people of your own culture and socioeconomic level. However, a church that takes such an approach misses out on many people who not only can help grow their church, but who can also enrich it spiritually. For instance, churches that learn to reach out to immigrants from third-world cultures often find that the strength of the faith of such people puts their own to shame. This is because their faith was often born and nurtured in an environment that was hostile to Christianity or that was economically or politically oppressive, and their faith had to become strong to survive their environment.

What does a church miss out on when its members only reach out to people of their own culture?

Churches that reach out only to those of their own culture also often die out quickly when the neighborhood in which they are situated starts to change and include mixed cultures.

What then should we as church members and leaders do? Here are some suggestions:

1. DISCOVER WHAT CULTURAL GROUPS ARE PRESENT IN THE COMMUNITY, BUT ARE UNDER-REPRESENTED IN THE CHURCHES. This can be done by checking community census data, available through the local chamber of commerce or city planning offices. Of course, sometimes there is a good reason for a cultural group being under-represented in the church. In many Asian cultures, for instance, people are predominately Buddhist. It would then be understandable that their culture would not be well represented in local churches. However, not only are there Christians who are a part of these cultures, but this can be a challenging mission opportunity to share Christ with Buddhists.

What is a good way to check out which cultural groups are present in your community?

2. INVITE SOMEONE FROM ANOTHER CULTURE INTO YOUR HOME. Get to know the person and some special facts about their culture or cultural values. What can you discover that you really like about their culture? This person does not have to be someone of another nationality. It could be someone who is from a different subculture—a different race or a counter-cultural young person.

3. INITIATE A PULPIT EXCHANGE, COMBINED WORSHIP, OR SOCIAL FUNCTION BETWEEN YOUR CHURCH AND AN ETHNIC CHURCH. Of course, if your church is an ethnic church, initiate a similar experience with a church of the dominant culture. If some church members don't speak the other's language, translations of the sermon and/or hymns need to be provided.

notes:

CARING TIME
Remain in groups of 6–8 people, in a horseshoe configuration.

Hand out the Prayer/Praise Report to the entire group. Ask each subgroup to pray for the empty chair. Pray specifically for God to guide you to someone to bring next week to fill that chair.

After a sufficient time of prayer in subgroups, close in a corporate prayer. Say, "Next week we will talk about: 'A Praying Church.' "

Remind participants of the daily Scripture readings and reflective questions found on page 61.

Caring Time (15-20 minutes)

6

Close by praying for one another. Begin this time by having each person answer the question,

"If you could receive an answer to just one question you are facing in your life, what would you want answered?"

Then pray for direction in regard to each other's questions. In addition, pray for the concerns on the Prayer/Praise Report.

notes:

BIBLE STUDY NOTES

Reference Notes

Use these notes to gain further understanding of the text as you study on your own:

ACTS 10:1
a centurion

Cornelius. The Romans typically used three names. Cornelius was a popular name taken on by the descendants of slaves who were released from slavery by the action of a P. Cornelius Sculla in 82 B.C. Cornelius would have been this soldier's middle name.
a centurion. Equivalent to the rank of an army captain in today's terms.
the Italian Regiment. An auxiliary force stationed in the area composed of men recruited from Italy.

ACTS 10:2
prayer and almsgiving

God-fearing. The distinction between Gentile God-fearers (who believed in the true God and obeyed His ethical commands) and proselytes (who fully converted to Judaism) lay in the hesitancy of the former to submit to the Jewish ceremonial laws, especially circumcision. Cornelius demonstrated his faith by practicing the Jewish disciplines of prayer and almsgiving.

ACTS 10:3

about three in the afternoon. This was the time for afternoon prayers at the temple in Jerusalem. Although Cornelius would never be able to participate fully in the temple services, he may have followed its pattern in terms of his own mode and time for prayer.

ACTS 10:4
devotion

Lord. Cornelius did not yet know of Jesus, so this is an expression of respect for what Cornelius recognized as a divine visitor.
as a memorial offering by God. Although Cornelius would not have been allowed to offer animal sacrifices in the temple, the angel lets him know that his heart-attitude of devotion to God is recognized as a real sacrifice that is acceptable to God.

ACTS 10:5–8

Told by the angel to send for Peter in Joppa, Cornelius sends three men to do so, at least one of whom shared his devotion to God.

ACTS 10:9

about noon. When apart from the temple, many devout Jews prayed at 9 a.m., noon, and 3 p.m. (Ps. 55:17).
up on the roof. Roofs were flat and often used as places for people to sit.

ACTS 10:14
invitation

Lord. Typically in Acts, this word is used as a title for Jesus. Peter may have recognized his dream as coming from the Lord, but he was not willing to simply follow the Lord's invitation to eat of the food.

ACTS 10:15
holiness

In Mark 7:19 Jesus laid the groundwork for the pronouncement that, despite the laws of Leviticus 11, food simply was not a spiritual issue. Such laws had their place earlier in Jewish history as a means of separating them from the pagans in neighboring areas, and as an object lesson about the meaning of holiness (that is, being separated out for God's use). (For an Old Testament story where eating became an issue for young Jewish men who sought to retain their cultural identity, read Daniel 1:3-17.)

ACTS 10:15
holiness
(cont'd)

However, Jesus' point was to show that these object lessons were not to be mistaken as God's ultimate concern: his interest was in genuine, inward holiness that had nothing to do with external matters such as food, circumcision, etc. Demonstrating the reality of this was the burden of much of Paul's ministry (Rom. 2:25-29; 14:13-18; 1 Cor. 8:4-13; Gal. 4:8-11; 5:6; Phil. 3:2-9). Peter soon came to see that if God can pronounce that certain foods that were formerly unclean are now acceptable, he can do the same thing with people. If it is now acceptable for Jews to eat the food of Gentiles, then the Gentiles themselves must be considered as acceptable to God as well.

ACTS 10:18
the rock

who was known as Peter. Jesus had renamed Simon "Peter," meaning "rock," because Jesus had foreseen that he would be the rock upon which the church would be built (Matt. 16:17-19).

ACTS 10:19
the vision

still thinking about the vision. Peter was no doubt trying to determine what the vision meant in terms of actions he should or should not take. While he was seeking such direction, God sent him the answer in the form of the centurion's messengers.

ACTS 10:20

I have sent them. The deity of the Spirit is shown here in that He speaks for God in the first person.

ACTS 10:22
God-fearer

The men speak of Cornelius in a way to present him as favorably as possible to Peter. He is a God-fearer, respected by the Jews in his community. Since it would not be easy for a Roman to earn such Jewish respect, this was particularly impressive. What is more, an angel spoke to him about Peter, saying that he should listen to whatever Peter had to say to him. Thus prepared, Peter would have to be expectant that something especially important was about to occur.

ACTS 10:23
hospitality

While Jews would offer Gentiles hospitality, they typically would refuse to accept it from Gentiles lest they violate dietary laws. Assuming the messengers arrived in early afternoon (v. 9), it would have been too late in the day to start the 30-mile journey back to Caesarea.

notes:

Session 7

A Praying Church

Prepare for the Session

	READINGS	REFLECTIVE QUESTIONS
Monday	Acts 12:1–4	In what ways are you like Herod, attempting to please the crowd?
Tuesday	Acts 12:5–11	From what has God rescued you? Whose prayers were part of helping this to happen?
Wednesday	Acts 12:12–17	In what frustrating areas of your life do you need to "keep on knocking"? How does God help you to persist in these circumstances?
Thursday	Acts 13:32–33	In what ways has God been faithful to His promises to you?
Friday	Acts 13:38–39	Meditate on how gracious God has been in forgiving you of your sins.
Saturday	Acts 13:49–52	In what ways do you need to "shake the dust" of a past failure from your feet and move on to what God is calling you to do next?
Sunday	Acts 14:1–3	How bold are you being in standing up for your Lord Jesus Christ?

notes:

OUR GOALS FOR THIS SESSION ARE:

In groups of 6–8, gather people in a horseshoe configuration.

Make sure everyone has a name tag.

Take time to share information on class parties that are coming up as well as any relevant church events.

INTRODUCE THE ICEBREAKER ACTIVITY: The students have been told in their books to choose one answer.

After the Icebreaker say something like, "Prayer opened many doors for the church of Acts—including the doors of some prisons. But surprisingly people didn't always burst right through those open doors. Rather, they were surprised by them. Understanding this story for today may keep us from likewise being surprised by the open doors that prayer provides us."

Hand out the Prayer/Praise Report. A sample copy is on pages 158-159. Have people write down prayer requests and praises. Then have the prayer coordinator collect the report and make copies for use during the Caring Time.

BIBLE STUDY
- to better understand the role that prayer played in the early church
- to appreciate the power of prayer to change things in our world
- to consider what our expectations of prayer should be and how those expectations influence prayer's effect

LIFE CHANGE
- to ask two people outside of the class to share a time when God responded to their prayers in a seemingly miraculous way
- to pray each day this week about some seemingly "impossible" situation
- to submit a previous prayer disappointment to Christ's Lordship

Icebreaker (10-15 minutes)

An Open Door. Go around the group on question 1 and let everyone share. Then go around again on question 2.

1. When you were in high school, which of the following "open doors" were you likely to burst right through and which ones were you likely to miss entirely? Mark the ones you would have taken advantage of right away with a "+" and those you would have missed with a "–":

___ Someone gave me the perfect lead-in for a put-down joke.
___ An attractive person of the opposite sex hinted they were interested in me.
___ A teacher gave me a chance to improve my grade.
___ I was given special encouragement to try out for the school play.
___ A good summer job suddenly became available.
___ I was given a chance to become a foreign exchange student.

notes:

Icebreaker (cont'd)

2. What door would you most like to see opened at this stage of your life?

- ☐ the door to a new career opportunity
- ☐ the door to a new friendship or love relationship
- ☐ the door to a promotion within my present career
- ☐ the door to an exciting travel opportunity
- ☐ the door to an exciting educational opportunity
- ☐ the door to a new understanding of myself
- ☐ other: ______________________________

notes:

LEARNING FROM THE BIBLE

ACTS 12:1-17

Have four members of the class, selected ahead of time, read the passage from Acts. One member should read the narrative portion; the second should read the part of the angel (vv. 7c, 8); the third the part of Peter (vv. 11, 17b); and the fourth the part of Rhoda (v. 14b). The whole class should read the reaction of the disciples (v. 15).

Bible Study (30-45 minutes)

The Scripture for this week:

*[1]It was about this time that King Herod arrested some who
belonged to the church, intending to persecute them. [2]He had James,
the brother of John, put to death with the sword. [3]When he saw that
this pleased the Jews, he proceeded to seize Peter also. This happened
during the Feast of Unleavened Bread. [4]After arresting him, he put
him in prison, handing him over to be guarded by four squads of four
soldiers each. Herod intended to bring him out for public trial after
the Passover.*

[5]So Peter was kept in prison, but the church was earnestly praying to God for him.

*[6]The night before Herod was to bring him to trial, Peter was
sleeping between two soldiers, bound with two chains, and sentries
stood guard at the entrance. [7]Suddenly an angel of the Lord
appeared and a light shone in the cell. He struck Peter on the side
and woke him up. "Quick, get up!" he said, and the chains fell off
Peter's wrists.*

[8]Then the angel said to him, "Put on your clothes and sandals." And Peter did so. "Wrap your cloak around you and follow me." the angel told him. [9]Peter followed him out of the prison, but he had no idea that what the angel was doing was really happening; he thought he was seeing a vision. [10]They passed the first and second guards and came to the iron gate leading to the city. It opened for them by itself, and they went through it. When they had walked the length of one street, suddenly the angel left him.

[11]Then Peter came to himself and said, "Now I know without a doubt that the Lord sent his angel and rescued me from Herod's clutches and from everything the Jewish people were anticipating."

[12]When this had dawned on him, he went to the house of Mary the mother of John, also called Mark, where many people had gathered and were praying. [13]Peter knocked at the outer entrance, and a servant girl named Rhoda came to answer the door. [14]When she recognized Peter's voice, she was so overjoyed she ran back without opening it and exclaimed, "Peter is at the door!"

[15]"You're out of your mind," they told her. When she kept insisting that it was so, they said, "It must be his angel."

[16]But Peter kept on knocking, and when they opened the door and saw him, they were astonished. [17]Peter motioned with his hand for them to be quiet and described how the Lord had brought him out of prison. "Tell James and the brothers about this," he said, and then he left for another place.

notes:

Summarize these introductory remarks. Be sure to include the underlined information, which gives the answers to the student book questions (provided in the margin).

What three different ways of looking at prayer are mentioned?

What example is given of a time in the Bible when God said "no" to an earnest prayer?

...about today's session (5 minutes)

THE POWER OF PRAYER

What role does prayer play in the church today? If some churches were honest about that question, they might say, "It starts and ends meetings." But is that all it is supposed to do? The church today seems to wrestle with what the role and power of prayer is. Some view it as a last-ditch effort after all the more practical efforts to change things fail. Others see it as simply a means to communicate with and submit to God, with no real power to change the course of events in our world.1 Still others see it as a kind of "magic wand" to make good things happen and all bad things go away.[2] In almost every church you can find people eager to testify to times God "answered" their prayers, and in almost every church—as well as in the secular world—you can find people who are disillusioned because an earnest prayer went "unanswered."

In the midst of this confusion, the Bible gives us some honest direction. It points out times when God said "no" to earnest prayers, as when Paul requested that a "thorn in my flesh" be removed (2 Cor. 12:7-9). But it also tells us that prayer can have great power to change things. Through prayer, Elijah changed weather patterns (Jas. 5:17-18). Through faith Jesus said it is possible to move mountains (Matt. 17:20–21). And as we will see in our story for today, through prayer Peter was miraculously freed from prison. Why prayer sometimes has a dramatic effect, and sometimes appears to have no effect, is what we will consider in today's session.

notes:

Remain in groups of 6–8 people, in a horseshoe configuration.

In this small-group session, students will be responding to the following questions that will help them share their stories in terms of the freeing of Peter from prison as described in Acts 12:1-17.

Have the students explore these questions together.

Identifying with the Story (5-7 minutes)

1. When you were a child in grade school and you had a story to tell that was hard to believe, who would generally believe you when nobody else would?

   - ☐ my mom
   - ☐ my dad
   - ☐ a sibling
   - ☐ a grandparent
   - ☐ a good friend
   - ☐ a special teacher

2. When has something happened to you that was so good you didn't know if it was real or if you were dreaming?

3. When has God surprised you with the way that He answered your prayers?

notes:

Share with your class the following information which you may modify according to your own perspectives and teaching needs. The answers to the student book questions (provided in the margin) are underlined.

today's session (15-20 minutes)

Prayer was an important part of the church of Acts, but even there people didn't always understand its potential, as we will see in today's Scripture passage. What these new Christians learned in this incident can be an important lesson for the church today as well.

A Church Under Pressure

The story starts with some ominous actions by King Herod. The "King Herod" referred to here was Herod Agrippa I, the grandson of Herod the Great, who ruled when Jesus was born (Matt. 2:1), and

7

today's session (cont'd)

Why was this Herod persecuting the church?

the nephew of Herod Antipas who governed Galilee during Jesus' ministry. Herod Agrippa I was popular with the Jews; some even wondered if he might be the Messiah who would free them from Rome. To further cultivate this popularity, he resumed the persecution of the church, which had ceased upon Paul's conversion (Acts 9:31). James, the brother of John and one of the sons of Zebedee, was killed with the sword under this persecution. Also, Peter was arrested. Verse 5 tells us, "So Peter was kept in prison, but the church was earnestly praying to God for him." They were a church under pressure, and in the midst of that pressure they turned to prayer. Let's look at the results of those prayers.

Why was Herod waiting until after the Passover to deal with Peter?

Herod's intent was eventually to have Peter also killed, as he had James. But he was waiting until "after the Passover," as such an execution during the Passover would have been seen as sacrilegious (Mark 14:2). He handed Peter over to "four squads of four soldiers each," one for each of four six-hour watches. Two soldiers were in the cell with Peter chained to their wrists, while the other two stood guard at the door. These intense security measures may have been implemented precisely to prevent any such "unexplainable" escape, such as the one that happened when the Sanhedrin had imprisoned Peter earlier (Acts 5:17-21).

God Intervenes

At this point, two things happened: (1) an "angel of the Lord" appeared; and (2) a light shone—the description of the light, a common symbol of divine glory, underscores that this was a miraculous intervention of God. This led to a series of supernatural events that aided the escape:

- chains fell off Peter's wrist
- the guards did not seem to be aware or respond
- Peter and the angel left the prison, which was undoubtedly locked
- an iron gate leading into the city opened of its own accord

Seeing all of these events, Peter concluded in verse 11, "Now I know without a doubt that the Lord sent His angel and rescued me from Herod's clutches and from everything the Jewish people were anticipating." Remember again that when "the Jewish people" are referred to in Acts it means the Jewish religious leadership, as Peter and most of the Christians were also Jewish.

Where did Peter go after he was released from prison?

After this miraculous release we are told that Peter immediately went to the home of Mary, the mother of John Mark. John Mark was the one who wrote the Gospel of Mark. The disciples had gathered there and were praying. What were they praying for? To answer that question, we only have to refer back to verse 5, "So Peter was kept in prison, but the church was earnestly praying to God for him."

Surprising Results

What happened then? Peter was greeted by a maid named Rhoda, who was also part of the Christian community. She was so stunned that she didn't even think to let Peter in. So, with the possibility that the Sanhedrin had already sent guards out looking for him, she left Peter standing outside at the gate! She reported Peter's presence, which the disciples did not believe. Thus, this event is similar to Christ's resurrection where the disciples did not believe the report of the women that Christ had been raised (Luke 24:5-11).

In summary, then, the disciples were gathered praying for a divine intervention to save Peter from what happened to James. God heard their prayers and sent an angel to deliver Peter safely to them. But when he arrived, these praying disciples did not believe what had happened.

We can imagine that the disciples had become very discouraged when Peter was arrested. He was one of their strongest leaders, the one Jesus had called the "rock." And Herod had many soldiers armed with all of the weaponry of the era, while they were unarmed. It's easy to imagine that someone in this situation probably said, "Well, there isn't much we can really do now, but pray." Do we say things like that today, implying that prayer is nothing more than the last-ditch effort of the desperate? Let's consider some other scriptural references concerning what we should expect. We could look at James 5:13-18, where James tells us that the prayer of a righteous person is "powerful and effective." Or we could read Matthew 7:7-11, where Jesus says, "Ask and it will be given to you; seek and you will find; knock and the door will be opened to you." Both of these passages tell us that powerful things can happen when we pray with faith.

What scriptural references are given to tell of the power of prayer?

However, we have to also look at another aspect of this issue. Sometimes God's answer to prayer is "no." The disciples probably also prayed for James, the Son of Zebedee. James did not get led out of prison—he was executed. In Acts, there is no predictable pattern of how God will work. Dorcas, a kindly but relatively insignificant woman (Acts 9:36-41) is raised from the dead while a bold, courageous man like Stephen is not. Paul had what he called "a thorn in the flesh," which he prayed to God to remove. But God told him "no" because through Paul's weakness, God's power could all the more be made evident (2 Cor. 12:7-9).

today's session (cont'd)

The bottom line on this issue seems to be that we should pray constantly for our needs, but remember that God is in control, not us. There will be times when God will show His great power, and we will praise God for that. But there will also be times when what we pray for will not happen. It doesn't mean God doesn't care. Nor does it mean that there was something wrong with us. It just means that God has another plan. If our prayers directed the world, then we would be God.

What we need to do then, is to pray with the_________ that God can change things through our prayers, but also with the _________ of understanding that God knows what is best.

What we need to do then, is to pray with the belief that God can change things through our prayers, but also with the humility of understanding that God knows what is best.

notes:

Remain in groups of 6–8 people, in a horseshoe configuration.

In this small-group session, students will be applying the lessons of the text to their own lives through the following questions.

The students were asked (in the student book) to choose an answer for each question and explain why.

Learning from the Story (5-7 minutes)

1. Had you been Peter, which of the events of this story would you have found most surprising?

   ☐ That they had arrested you in the first place.
   ☐ That you were so miraculously freed from the prison.
   ☐ That Rhoda left you at the door instead of letting you in.
   ☐ other: ______________________________

2. Why do you think God delivered Peter from prison, but not James (v. 2)?

   ☐ God had more need of Peter's leadership.
   ☐ The people prayed more for Peter.
   ☐ God just wanted to demonstrate His power and chose Peter to do it with.
   ☐ Peter had greater faith.
   ☐ other: ______________________________

3. What do you think was the most important effect this event had on the life of the church in Jerusalem?
   - ☐ They had a new belief in the power of prayer.
   - ☐ They had a new confidence that the authorities couldn't defeat them.
   - ☐ They were reassured that they were on "the right side."
   - ☐ other: ______________________________

notes:

Share with the class the following thoughts on how the lessons of this text might be applied today. The answers to the student book questions (provided in the margin) are underlined unless the question requires a personal answer.

What two extremes do we need to avoid regarding our attitude about prayer results?

During times when our prayers aren't answered in the way we want, what words from Eli, in the book of Samuel, are we called upon to repeat?

life change lessons (5-7 minutes)

How should the story of Peter's release affect how we pray as individuals and as churches? What does this story mean in terms of practical action? Just as the Lord taught His disciples to pray (Luke 11:1-4), so we also need to be taught what attitude to have about the results of our prayers. We need to avoid the two extremes: (1) lack of belief that prayer has an effect, and (2) the naive prayer will be the magic wand with which we control the world. Behaviorally, the best way to keep things in proper perspective is with actions that balance each other. Backpackers know that a balanced load is easier to carry than an unbalanced one, and that is what we seek here. Here are some suggestions that when taken together can do just that:

7

1. ASK TWO PEOPLE OUTSIDE OF THE CLASS TO SHARE A TIME WHEN GOD RESPONDED TO THEIR PRAYERS IN A SEEMINGLY MIRACULOUS WAY. The more such instances we hear about, the more confidence we will have in the power of prayer. You may want to ask your pastor for suggestions on whom to ask.

2. PRAY EACH DAY THIS WEEK ABOUT SOME SEEMINGLY "IMPOSSIBLE" SITUATION. It may be someone who has a terminal disease, or a problem that has defied solution. Remember here that God does sometimes answer prayer with a "no," but don't let this keep you from asking. James has told us that often we do not have because we do not ask (Jas. 4:2-3).

3. SUBMIT A PREVIOUS PRAYER DISAPPOINTMENT TO CHRIST'S LORDSHIP. This may be a time when you prayed that a loved one would recover, and they didn't, or that you would get a job that went to someone else. As you recall this time, repeat the words Eli said in 1 Samuel 3:18: "He is the LORD; let him do what is good in his eyes."

CARING TIME
Remain in groups of 6–8 people, in a horseshoe configuration.

Hand out the Prayer/Praise Report to the entire group. Ask each subgroup to pray for the empty chair. Pray specifically for God to guide you to someone to bring next week to fill that chair.

After a sufficient time of prayer in subgroups, close in a corporate prayer. Say, "Next week we will talk about: 'Treated as Gods.' "

Remind participants of the daily Scripture readings and reflective questions found on page 71.

Caring Time (15-20 minutes)

Take time now to care for one another through prayer. Begin by having each group member answer the following question:

"From what 'prison' do you need to be released right now?"

Close by praying for one another. Also, use the Prayer/Praise Report and pray for the concerns and requests listed.

notes:

BIBLE STUDY NOTES

Reference Notes

Use these notes to gain further understanding of the text as you study on your own:

ACTS 12:1 ***persecution***

King Herod. This is Herod Agrippa I, the grandson of Herod the Great, who ruled when Jesus was born, and the nephew of Herod Antipas who governed Galilee during Jesus' ministry. Herod Agrippa I was popular with the Jews; some even wondered if he might be the Messiah who would free them from Rome. To further cultivate this popularity, he resumed the persecution of the church, which had ceased upon Paul's conversion (9:31). Since Herod died in A.D. 44, this story precedes the visit of Paul and Barnabas to Jerusalem (11:27-30).

ACTS 12:7 ***divine glory***

a light shone. Similarities between this story and other escape stories circulating in the first century have led some commentators to assume that supernatural overtones were added to an account of how Peter was released with the help of a sympathetic insider. However, this fails to account for how the security measures used to imprison Peter could have been circumvented. Peter was constantly guarded by four soldiers on six-hour shifts (vv. 4,6). Two soldiers were in the cell with Peter chained to their wrists, while the other two stood guard at the door. Such intense

ACTS 12:7
divine glory
(cont'd)

security measures may have been implemented to prevent any such "unexplainable" release such as happened when the Sanhedrin had imprisoned him earlier (5:19-24). The description of the light, a common symbol of divine glory, underscores that this was a miraculous intervention of God.

ACTS 12:8–10

In a trance-like state, Peter was led past the prison's guard and through the main door of the prison.

ACTS 12:11
mystery of God's ways

the Lord ... rescued me from Herod's clutches. In Acts, there is no predictable pattern of how God will work. While Peter was released from prison, James, for whom the church undoubtedly prayed just as earnestly, was killed. Dorcas, a kindly but relatively insignificant woman (9:36-41), is raised from the dead while a bold, courageous man like Stephen is not. Even in this account, Peter, although so miraculously protected by God, decides he should go into hiding lest Herod catch him again (v. 17). The answer to why these things should be so is not given. The mystery is only known in the secret counsel of God who works all things according to His will. The call to the church is to be faithful and take responsible action whether or not God chooses to act in a miraculous way.

ACTS 12:12

Mary the mother of John, also called Mark. This is the Mark who later wrote the Gospel bearing that name (12:25; 13:5).

ACTS 12:13–17

In a humorous way, Luke recounts how Peter was left standing at the gate of the courtyard while the disciples refused to believe that he could possibly be there!

ACTS 12:15
Peter's angel

It must be his angel. It was believed that each person had a guardian angel who watched over that individual. Assuming that Peter was killed, the only solution the disciples could come up with was that Peter's angel had taken on Peter's form.

ACTS 12:17
devotion to God

James. This is the half-brother of Jesus (Mark 6:3). James did not believe in Jesus as the Messiah during Jesus' ministry (John 7:5), but after the resurrection Jesus appeared to him in a special way (1 Cor. 15:7), qualifying James to be an apostle. James became a leader in the Jerusalem church (15:13; 21:18; Gal. 2:9), and his piety and devotion to God gained the respect of the Jewish community in general. When executed by the Sadducean high priest in A.D. 61, his death was mourned by many Pharisaic Jews as well as Christians.

he left for another place. While Peter recognized his release as an act of God, he did not believe that made him invulnerable to Herod's plots. Thus, he left Jerusalem for some time. Although Peter was in Jerusalem at the time of the council in Acts 15, nothing more is told of his story in Acts. Church tradition associates him with travels to Alexandria, Asia Minor, and finally Rome where he was crucified upside down by the Emperor Nero.

[1] This is essentially the view in the classic book by Harold Kushner, *When Bad Things Happen to Good People* (New York: Avon, 1981).

[2] For an interesting article that wrestles with this "magic wand" issue, see Chris Lutes, "First Church of Signs and Wonders," *Christianity Today*, January 8, 2001 p. 81.

Session

8

Treated as Gods

Prepare for the Session

	READINGS	REFLECTIVE QUESTIONS
Monday	Acts 14:8–10	Consider what "spiritual disabilities" you have at this point in your life. Do you have faith that God can heal you?
Tuesday	Acts 14:11–15	Have you made peace with the fact that you are only human?
Wednesday	Acts 14:16–18	How has God shown kindness to you? How have you thanked Him?
Thursday	Acts 14:19–20	When the world has seemingly turned against you, who has been there to help you pick up the pieces?
Friday	Acts 14:21–22	What hardships are you experiencing because you are seeking the kingdom of God? Who has encouraged you in the midst of those hardships?
Saturday	Acts 14:23–25	Is your trust truly in the Lord?
Sunday	Acts 14:26–28	For whom can you "open the door of faith"?

notes:

OUR GOALS FOR THIS SESSION ARE:

In groups of 6–8, gather people in a horseshoe configuration.

Make sure everyone has a name tag.

Take time to share information on class parties that are coming up as well as any relevant church events.

INTRODUCE THE ICEBREAKER ACTIVITY: The students have been told in their books to choose one answer.

After the Icebreaker say something like, "Having shared what we experienced this week in our own life's journey, we will now look at an instance in the journey of missionaries Paul and Barnabas. Just as our journeys have included ups and downs, so did theirs—sometimes all within one day. We will see how this happened."

Hand out the Prayer/Praise Report. A sample copy is on pages 158-159. Have people write down prayer requests and praises. Then have the prayer coordinator collect the report and make copies for use during the Caring Time.

BIBLE STUDY	• to look at the human tendency to view certain charismatic leaders as "gods" • to consider the humble way Paul and Barnabas dealt with the power given to them • to understand how quickly people can change their minds about whom they idolize
LIFE CHANGE	• to review the stories of Jim Jones and David Koresh • to make a list of positive and negative things you notice about Christian leaders in general • to become part of or remain in a group where honesty and openness is encouraged

Icebreaker (10-15 minutes)

This Week's Journey. Paul had many interesting experiences on his journeys. What about you? Imagine your journey this past week was a section of the trail that goes along a mountain range.

1. When did the "trail" seem so steep that you wished you could turn around and go back?

2. What beauty did you experience that made it, at least for the moment, seem all worthwhile?

3. Whom did you meet along the trail who made the hike the enjoyable?

4. What did you learn on this week's hike that will help you during the next few days of your trip?

8

notes:

LEARNING FROM THE BIBLE

ACTS 14:8-20

Have three members of the class, selected ahead of time, read the passage from Acts. Have one member read the part of Paul (vv. 10a, 15-17), one member read the part of Barnabas (vv. 15-17, with Paul), and one member the narration. Have the whole class read the part of the crowd (v. 11b).

Bible Study (30-45 minutes)

The Scripture for this week:

[8]In Lystra there sat a man crippled in his feet, who was lame from
birth and had never walked. [9]He listened to Paul as he was speaking.
Paul looked directly at him, saw that he had faith to be healed [10]and
called out, "Stand up on your feet!" At that, the man jumped up and
began to walk.

[11]When the crowd saw what Paul had done, they shouted in the
Lycaonian language, "The gods have come down to us in human
form!" [12]Barnabas they called Zeus, and Paul they called Hermes
because he was the chief speaker. [13]The priest of Zeus, whose temple
was just outside the city, brought bulls and wreaths to the city gates
because he and the crowd wanted to offer sacrifices to them.

[14]But when the apostles Barnabas and Paul heard of this, they
tore their clothes and rushed out into the crowd, shouting: [15]"Men,
why are you doing this? We too are only men, human like you. We
are bringing you good news, telling you to turn from these worthless
things to the living God, who made heaven and earth and sea and
everything in them. [16]In the past, he let all nations go their own way.
[17]Yet he has not left himself without testimony: He has shown kind-
ness by giving you rain from heaven and crops in their seasons; he
provides you with plenty of food and fills your hearts with joy."
[18]Even with these words, they had difficulty keeping the crowd from
sacrificing to them.

[19]Then some Jews came from Antioch and Iconium and won the
crowd over. They stoned Paul and dragged him outside the city,
thinking he was dead. [20]But after the disciples had gathered around
him, he got up and went back into the city. The next day he and
Barnabas left for Derbe.

notes:

Summarize these introductory remarks. Be sure to include the underlined information, which gives the answers to the student book questions (provided in the margin).

What ancient peoples deified their leaders?

What leader in recent times did people treat like a "god"?

...about today's session (5 minutes)

THE ONE TRUE GOD

In all areas of life, we as humans seem to have an overwhelming need to deify each other. Ancient Egypt and Rome epitomized this tendency, officially declaring their Pharaohs and Caesars to be gods. We call this ancient superstition, but in reality we do the same thing. Hitler was able to accomplish his evil acts because the German people essentially gave him divine power and asked him to be their "savior." Every election year in the United States, die-hard loyalists promote their own candidate as the next savior for the world's problems. But it's not just in politics that this happens. Jim Jones and David Koresh have shown us how religious leaders can be seen as gods. That there exists a "Church of Elvis" is enough to remind us how this deification occurs with entertainment figures as well.

Why do we have this need to deify each other? Perhaps it's to buoy up our own inadequacy and vulnerability in the world. Perhaps it's to fill a gap we leave when we can't submit to the true God. In any case, it is a tendency that people had in Paul's day as well. When Paul and Barnabas used the power of Jesus Christ to heal someone, one town was ready to deify them, even though it was against their will. As we look at the story of how this happened, we might be able to gain new understanding as to why it happens today as well.

notes:

8

Remain in groups of 6–8 people, in a horseshoe configuration.

In this small-group session, students will be responding to the following questions that will help them share their stories in terms of the deification of Paul and Barnabas.

Have the students explore these questions together.

Identifying with the Story (5-7 minutes)

1. When you were in school, who were you most likely to think of as "gods"?
   - ☐ baseball players like Mickey Mantle, Willie Mays, George Brett, or Pete Rose
   - ☐ basketball players like Wilt Chamberlain, Larry Bird, or Michael Jordan
   - ☐ football players like Gayle Sayers, Joe Montana, John Elway, or Emmitt Smith
   - ☐ singers like Elvis Presley, Aretha Franklin, Prince, or Madonna
   - ☐ actors like Gregory Peck, John Wayne, Jane Fonda, Harrison Ford, or Julia Roberts
   - ☐ political leaders like Bobby Kennedy, Ronald Reagan, Geraldine Ferraro, or Diane Feinstein
   - ☐ religious leaders like Billy Graham, Rick Warren, Mother Teresa, or the Pope
2. Finish this sentence: "The last time I felt I was really treated 'like a god' was when ..."
3. In general, do you feel people treat you better than you deserve, as the Lycaonians did with Paul and Barnabas at first; or worse than you deserve, as they treated Paul and Barnabas after the Jewish instigators came along?

notes:

Share with your class the following information which you may modify according to your own perspectives and teaching needs. The answers to the student book questions (provided in the margin) are underlined.

According to local legend, what two Greek gods had already come down to earth in this region in human form?

Why didn't Paul and Barnabas understand at first that they were being thought of as gods come to earth in human form?

today's session (15-20 minutes)

Paul and his companions relied on the power of God to do great things. As a result, great things happened. But this, in turn, meant that some people mistook the power of God working through them for them actually being gods. The event where this happened occurred in Lystra on Paul's first missionary journey. Lystra was the hometown of Timothy (Acts 16:1-2). There were two local legends here that told of times when Zeus and Hermes had come down in human likeness: (1) Lycaon entertained these gods by feasting them on human flesh, and was turned into a wolf for doing so; (2) Baucis and Philemon, an elderly couple, were the only people who welcomed the gods, and were rewarded by being allowed to die at the same time so neither would have to mourn the other. This is important background information that helps us to understand why the people here were so quick to declare Paul and Barnabas to be the gods Zeus and Hermes.

A Miraculous Healing

What happened at this place? Paul healed a man who had been lame since birth. As we look at the story we see an interesting phrase declaring that Paul, "saw that he had faith to be healed" (v. 9). How did he see this? Did he show it in a positive demeanor, in how he treated the people around him, or in the statements of faith he was making? Perhaps all of the above. In any case, we consistently see in Scripture that faith is a necessary element in healing.

When this healing happened the people got excited and started speaking in their native tongue, Lycaonian, rather than in the Greek that Paul was speaking. Because of this, Paul and the others probably didn't understand at first what they were saying. Their initial statement was, "The gods have come down to us in human form!" (v. 11). They believed that their legends were coming true once again. Barnabas they called Zeus because he may have been considered the leader of this mission. (See Acts 13:2 and 13:7.) In both of these verses the name of Barnabas is mentioned first, indicating that when the mission first started Paul may have been seen as of secondary importance to Barnabas. Zeus was the chief of the gods, and Barnabas was the one they saw as being like him. Hermes was the patron god of oratory, and they gave Paul this name because "he was the chief speaker" (v. 12).

8

A Reaction of Shock

In verse 13, we find that people came from the temple of Zeus outside the city and wanted to offer sacrifice. All of this must have taken some time. Verse 14 tells us that when Paul and Barnabas

today's session (cont'd)

Why did Paul and Barnabas tear their clothes?

heard of it they tore their clothes. This was a sign of repentance and mourning. They were shocked that people were treating them as gods, and didn't want there to be any thought that they were encouraging such a practice. They were there to teach about the true God, and they wanted no part of idolatry, especially if *they* were being made into the idols.

After they realize that they are being thought of as gods, what three points do Paul and Barnabas make to the crowd?

Paul and Barnabas say some important things in their speech to the crowd: (1) they are only human; (2) the people should turn to the one and only God; and (3) that there is a true God who created all that is, and that he had always sought to speak to them through the natural world. (Compare Rom. 1:19-20.) They could have also added that God had come to earth in human form, as the Lycaonians had said (v. 11), only it wasn't their human form, it was the human form of Jesus of Nazareth. Even after their speech, the people still wanted to treat them as if they were gods (v. 18).

Letting People be People

What do we learn from this for our time? The message of Paul and Barnabas is still valid for us: (1) We need to let humans just be humans. When we try to turn them into gods, we set them up to fall and we dishonor the One who truly is God. No human being can "save" us. There is a song that Tina Turner sang called, "We Don't Need Another Hero." That title says it well. Christ alone is our Savior and we don't need anyone else; (2) It follows then that we should turn to the one and only God. Only the true God, the Father of our Lord Jesus Christ, can help us find our true place in the creation. That is because ...; (3) God is indeed the Creator of all that is. Because of that, He knows how we fit into His creation. Christian psychologist, Paul Tournier writes, "I see this complicated human machine as a great organ, with all its registers, its stops and its pipes. But according to whom you get to play it, you will get a frightening cacophony, or marvelous heavenly music! ... A civilization which has dismissed the organist, which believes only in nature, only in the virtue of the machine, has invited the rising generation to make it work at random amid deafening noise. ... The organ is meant for the organist, and without him it has no meaning."[1]

To what does Paul Tournier liken those who try to function without the direction of their Creator?

What are we encouraged to do instead of relying on one "godlike" charismatic leader?

For the church, this means that we need to accept our pastors and Christian leaders as persons with weaknesses and flaws. What we need is not someone who appears strong and perfect, but one who knows that God's grace is the cure for our human weakness. Rather than relying on one "godlike" charismatic leader, we need to rely on the church as a whole for direction and support. God gives us the church for support and direction, but the church is more than one person. The senior pastor might help us by giving us a new insight, while a Sunday school teacher might help us solve a problem with which we have been wrestling, and a young child might give us a reassuring hug! When we realize that everyone in the church can be an important spiritual resource for us, we can better resist the idea of idolizing just one person.

notes:

Remain in groups of 6–8 people, in a horseshoe configuration.

In this small-group session, students will be applying the lessons of the text to their own lives through the following questions.

The students were asked (in the student book) to choose an answer for each question and explain why.

Learning from the Story (5-7 minutes)

1. Why was the crowd that had previously proclaimed Paul and Barnabas as gods so quickly persuaded to stone them?

2. Why were Paul and Barnabas so upset when they realized the crowd was getting ready to offer sacrifices to them?

   - ☐ They thought God might punish them.
   - ☐ They knew God alone was worthy of such behavior.
   - ☐ People weren't listening to their message about Jesus.
   - ☐ They didn't want people expecting too much of them.
   - ☐ other:____________________

3. What do you see as the most significant message Barnabas and Saul sought to deliver to the crowd?

   - ☐ There is one living God for all people (v. 15).
   - ☐ God is the Creator of everything (v. 15).
   - ☐ God had always reached out to them (v. 17).
   - ☐ God provided for them materially (v. 17).
   - ☐ God provided for them spiritually and emotionally (v. 17).

8

Share with the class the following thoughts on how the lessons of this text might be applied today. The answers to the student book questions (provided in the margin) are underlined unless the question requires a personal answer.

"We need to let people be ________."

What might be one possible reason that some people see only the negative in others?

life change lessons (5-7 minutes)

Putting this week's lesson into action might necessitate changing the way we relate to people. No more putting people up on a pedestal. No more expecting human beings to save us. No more ignoring flaws in order to maintain the pristine image we have of someone. We need to let people be <u>people</u>. For some of us that will be easier than for others. Some do the opposite and see the worst in everyone, and that is not letting people be people either. The negative is blown out of proportion and we forget to see the image of God in the people around us. <u>Sometimes this behavior comes from expecting too much of someone and being let down</u>.

All of us can benefit from some disciplines. Here are some specific suggestions:

1. REVIEW THE STORIES OF JIM JONES AND DAVID KORESH. These can be found in any library. Reminding ourselves of what happened in these incidents can help keep us from letting it happen again.
2. MAKE A LIST OF THE POSITIVE AND NEGATIVE THINGS YOU NOTICE ABOUT CHRISTIAN LEADERS IN GENERAL. This should include at least three positive and three negative things. It should only be for yourself. The purpose is to help you see these influential spiritual leaders as a human being, and neither a god nor a demon.
3. BECOME PART OF OR REMAIN IN A GROUP WHERE HONESTY AND OPENNESS IS ENCOURAGED. This group could be this class or perhaps a small committed group that meets in homes. It needs to be a place where members let themselves be known, "moles and all." Being a part of such a group helps keep us from idolizing others or from trying to get them to see us in an idealistic way.

CARING TIME
Remain in groups of 6–8 people, in a horseshoe configuration.

Hand out the Prayer/Praise Report to the entire group. Ask each subgroup to pray for the empty chair. Pray specifically for God to guide you to someone to bring next week to fill that chair.

After a sufficient time of prayer in subgroups, close in a corporate prayer. Say, "Next week we will talk about: 'Dealing with the Old Laws.' "

Remind participants of the daily Scripture readings and reflective questions found on page 79.

Caring Time (15-20 minutes)

Take this time to encourage one another in prayer. Begin by having each group member answer the question:

"What has God done recently that has 'filled your heart with joy' (v. 17)?"

Thank God for these things in prayer. In addition, pray for the concerns on the Prayer/Praise Report.

BIBLE STUDY NOTES

Reference Notes

Use these notes to gain further understanding of the text as you study on your own:

ACTS 14:8
new strategy

The small Jewish community in Lystra (16:1-3) apparently did not have a synagogue. Adopting a new strategy that brought the gospel directly to the Gentiles, Paul probably preached in the Greek forum, the site of the local marketplace and gathering place for public discussion.

ACTS 14:11
legend

An ancient legend said that Jupiter and Mercury (the Latin counterparts to Zeus and Hermes) appeared to a couple in a nearby area. As a result, the local people made pilgrimages to this site and the worship of these gods flourished in the region through the third century A.D.

ACTS 14:12
herald

Hermes ... the chief speaker. Zeus was the chief god among the Greek deities, while Hermes was the herald of the gods. The fact that Paul was identified with Hermes shows that he was the leading speaker in this missionary enterprise.

ACTS 14:14
grief

they tore their clothes. In the ancient world, this was a universally recognized sign of horror and grief. By so doing, the missionaries demonstrate the intensity of their opposition to what the people were supposedly doing in their honor.

ACTS 14:15–17
one God

Paul declares that he and Barnabas are in no way divine, but only human messengers bringing a message from the one true, living God.

ACTS 14:19–20
Jewish zealots

Although there was not a sufficient Jewish community in Lystra to cause any opposition, some traditional Jewish zealots who had traveled from Antioch (over 150 miles away) and Iconium reflected Paul's former zeal in opposing the gospel by traveling to Lystra to stir up the people against him.

ACTS 14:20
Paul revived

he got up. While some consider this a miracle or resurrection, Luke gives no indication that this was so. Paul was badly beaten and bruised, but able to travel on to Derbe. Paul refers to this incident in 2 Corinthians 11:25 with no mention of any miraculous resurrection or recovery.

notes:

[1] Paul Tournier, *The Violence Within* (San Francisco: Harper & Row, 1977), pp. 77–78.

Session

9 Dealing with the Old Laws

Prepare for the Session

	READINGS	REFLECTIVE QUESTIONS
Monday	Acts 15:1–5	What "law" do you still feel you need to fulfill to "measure up"? How completely has God's grace struck home to you?
Tuesday	Acts 15:6–11	When was the last time you told someone what God has done for you and through you? Who could you tell today?
Wednesday	Acts 15:12–21	In what way is your lifestyle making it easier, or more difficult, for others to believe?
Thursday	Acts 15:24–29	What have you risked for Jesus Christ?
Friday	Acts 15:30–35	To whom have you given an encouraging message recently? To whom do you need to give an encouraging message?
Saturday	Acts 15:36	What Christian brother or sister do you need to contact and "see how they are doing"? Should you call, send a letter, or e-mail?
Sunday	Acts 15:37–41	How are you doing at giving others a second chance?

notes:

OUR GOALS FOR THIS SESSION ARE:

BIBLE STUDY	• to consider the importance of the controversy over circumcision in the early church • to gain a better understanding of the place of Old Testament laws and traditions • to appreciate how the controversy over circumcision was dealt with, and its implications for handling church conflict
LIFE CHANGE	• to interview our pastor or other influential church teacher on the role of Old Testament law and tradition in the life of the Christian • to talk with a friend and discover his understanding of Old Testament law • to write out a statement of our own view on the applicability of Old Testament law for the Christian

In groups of 6–8, gather people in a horseshoe configuration.

Make sure everyone has a name tag.

Take time to share information on class parties that are coming up as well as any relevant church events.

INTRODUCE THE ICEBREAKER ACTIVITY: The students have been told in their books to choose one answer.

After the Icebreaker, say something like, "The 'house rules' in the home in which we were raised have affected each one of us. They also affected the early church. Their 'house rules' were the Old Testament laws and traditions, and in order to grow the church had to first deal with these old rules. In today's session we will see how they did this."

Hand out the Prayer/Praise Report. A sample copy is on pages 158-159. Have people write down prayer requests and praises. Then have the prayer coordinator collect the report and make copies for use during the Caring Time.

Icebreaker (10-15 minutes)

House Rules. Go around the group on question 1 and let everyone share. Then go around again on question 2.

1. What were some of the "house rules," written and unwritten, in the home where you were raised?

- ☐ "Don't rock the boat."
- ☐ "Father knows best!"
- ☐ "If Mom ain't happy; ain't nobody happy!"
- ☐ "Don't talk to others about family business."
- ☐ "Don't talk back."
- ☐ "Don't run in the house."
- ☐ "Children should be seen and not heard."
- ☐ "Clean up after yourself."
- ☐ "You use it; you put it away."
- ☐ "Don't say, 'Shut up!' "
- ☐ "Do what you want, but stay out of my way."
- ☐ "Walk softly when Dad's home."

2. What was your attitude toward "house rules" when you were an adolescent? Rate yourself on the following scale:

1 . . . . 2 . . . . 3 . . . . 4 5

My parents said "jump," and I said, "How high?" — Whatever my parents said, I did the opposite.

LEARNING FROM THE BIBLE

ACTS 15:1-21

Have five members of the class, selected ahead of time, read the passage from Acts. Have two members read the part of those advocating circumcision (vv. 1b, 5a); one member read the part of Peter (vv. 7b-11); one member read the part of James (vv. 13b-21); and one member the narration.

Bible Study (30-45 minutes)

The Scripture for this week:

[1]Some men came down from Judea to Antioch and were teaching
the brothers: "Unless you are circumcised, according to the custom
taught by Moses, you cannot be saved." [2]This brought Paul and
Barnabas into sharp dispute and debate with them. So Paul and
Barnabas were appointed, along with some other believers, to go up
to Jerusalem to see the apostles and elders about this question. [3]The
church sent them on their way, and as they traveled through
Phoenicia and Samaria they told how the Gentiles had been converted.
This news made all the brothers very glad. [4]When they came to
Jerusalem, they were welcomed by the church and the apostles and
elders, to whom they reported everything God had done through him.
[5]Then some of the believers who belonged to the party of the
Pharisees stood up and said, "The Gentiles must be circumcised and
required to obey the law of Moses."
[6]The apostles and elders met to consider this question. [7]After
much discussion, Peter got up and addressed them: "Brothers, you
know that some time ago God made a choice among you that the
Gentiles might hear from my lips the message of the gospel and
believe. [8]God, who knows the heart, showed that he accepted them
by giving the Holy Spirit to them, just as he did to us. [9]He made no
distinction between us and them, for he purified their hearts by faith.
[10]Now then, why do you try to test God by putting on the necks of the
disciples a yoke that neither we nor our fathers have been able to
bear? [11]No! We believe it is through the grace of our Lord Jesus that
we are saved, just as they are."
[12]The whole assembly became silent as they listened to Barnabas
and Paul telling about the miraculous signs and wonders God had
done among the Gentiles through them. [13]When they finished, James
spoke up: "Brothers, listen to me. [14]Simon has described to us how
God at first showed his concern by taking from the Gentiles a people
for himself. [15]The words of the prophets are in agreement with this, as
it is written:

> *[16]" 'After this I will return*
> *and rebuild David's fallen tent.*
> *Its ruins I will rebuild,*
> *and I will restore it,*

> [17]*that the remnant of men may seek the Lord,*
> *and all the Gentiles who bear my name,*
> *says the Lord, who does these things'*
> [18]*that have been known for ages.*
>
> [19]*"It is my judgment, therefore, that we should not make it difficult for the Gentiles who are turning to God.* [20]*Instead we should write to them, telling them to abstain from food polluted by idols, from sexual immorality, from the meat of strangled animals and from blood.* [21]*For Moses has been preached in every city from the earliest times and is read in the synagogues on every Sabbath."*

notes:

Summarize these introductory remarks. Be sure to include the underlined information, which gives the answers to the student book questions (provided in the margin).

What example is given of a law that now seems trivial because it no longer serves its original function?

...about today's session (5 minutes)

9

GOD'S GRACE UNITES US

When people talk about trivial laws, one that is often mentioned is the law against spitting on the sidewalk. Most people would say that such a law sounds rather trivial. However, these laws came into being when tuberculosis was as frightening a disease as AIDS is today. We learn that saliva was considered a way of spreading the disease, then we realize that, in its day, the law had a serious purpose. Of course today, since TB is extremely rare in our society, such laws no longer seem as appropriate.

In a similar way, the matter of whether followers of Christ should be circumcised seems like a trivial matter today. Isn't it just a matter of a health choice? And yet this was one of the most divisive issues

...about today's session (cont'd)

Why was it important in Old Testament times for Jewish men to have a sign that they were different from men of other cultures?

in the early church. The problem was that some people weren't able to recognize when the Law no longer served its original function. Originally circumcision separated Jewish men from the pagan cultures around them. Jewish men were to be different. That was important since men of other cultures often went in to prostitutes who were part of a fertility cult. Circumcision was a sign on the male sexual organ that they belonged to God and would have no part in this practice. Over time, however, it became less a sign of commitment to the true God and more a cultural emblem. Circumcision meant that you were part of Jewish culture. Many Gentile male "God-fearers" resisted full conversion to Judaism because they didn't want to be circumcised, and in a sense betray their culture. Circumcision had become a symbol of cultural division.

Jesus Christ came to bring people together in the kingdom of God. As Paul noted, "there is neither Jew nor Greek" (Gal. 3:28). All would have equal access to God through grace. In that context, symbols of what divided them no longer had a purpose.

Today we also need to learn to recognize when an old law or tradition no longer serves the purpose for which it was established. And above all we need to look to the grace of God that unites us. That is what this session is about.

Remain in groups of 6–8 people, in a horseshoe configuration.

In this small-group session, students' responses to the following questions will help them share their stories in terms of the dispute over circumcision.

Have the students explore these questions together.

Identifying with the Story (5-7 minutes)

1. What is most likely to cause "sharp disputes" in your church?
   - ☐ theological issues—like how to apply Scripture
   - ☐ worship music disputes—guitars vs. organ
   - ☐ personality issues—pro-pastor vs. anti-pastor
   - ☐ matters of church decor—like the color of the carpet
   - ☐ power struggles—"us" vs. "them"

2. In matters of church dispute, what is your most frequent approach?
   - ☐ "Let's not talk about anything that will make people mad."
   - ☐ "If they don't straighten up, I'll leave!"
   - ☐ "You have a right to your opinion—even if it is wrong!"
   - ☐ "Let's agree to disagree."
   - ☐ "As long as we keep talking and listening, we'll figure it out."
   - ☐ other: ______________________________

3. What church dispute has disturbed you the most?

notes:

today's session (15-20 minutes)

Share with your class the following information which you may modify according to your own perspectives and teaching needs. The answers to the student book questions (provided in the margin) are underlined.

With the growing mission to the Gentiles, especially through the work of Paul and his missionary team, a conflict also grew. Should the Gentile converts be required to perform the ritual acts of the Law that Jews had been required to do for centuries, particularly circumcision of males? In part, this controversy came about because this was a time of less differentiation between Christian and Jew. Those Jews who believed in Christ did not think they had converted to a new religion—they believed they had found the one their faith had been looking to for some time. As a result, they still held to many of the Jewish ways as essential. Paul and his Gentile converts saw no need for this, since Paul taught that Jesus brought freedom from the old Jewish law.

The First Church Council

What did the meeting at Jerusalem later become known as?

What creeds came out of later church councils?

To address this controversy, all the leaders of the church met together in what has since come to be known as the First Church Council. In the centuries to come there would be a number of such councils convened in order to decide on matters of correct doctrine in the face of ideas that were thought to be heretical. It was out of such councils that came what we know today as the Nicene Creed and the Apostles' Creed.

today's session (cont'd)

How was it possible that people who believed in Jesus Christ could still consider themselves to be Pharisees?

In this particular council the item of contention was this matter of circumcision of Gentiles. We note in verse 5 that some believers still aligned themselves with the Pharisees. Again this shows that the people of the time hadn't seen themselves as joining a new religion when they became followers of Christ, so they retained their allegiance to the Jewish sect that they had been part of previously. Remember, the Pharisees believed in all of the books we count as the Hebrew Scriptures (in contrast to the Sadducees who only believed in the first five books of the Old Testament), and they believed in angels and life after death. Therefore, even though Jesus had many conflicts with Pharisees over their extreme emphasis on adherence to the Law, the Pharisees still had many beliefs in common with Jesus.

Peter's Role

Peter here is a voice for the Gentiles. We might at first think it strange that Peter should describe his role, saying, "God made a choice among you that the Gentiles might hear from my lips the message of the gospel and believe" (v. 7). After all, Paul was there and he surely had much more involvement in spreading the gospel to the Gentiles. Still, Peter was the first to break this important barrier. As we remember from a previous session, Peter had his heart opened by a vision (Acts 10).

The key verse in regard to Peter's argument is in verse 10 where he asks, "why do you try to test God by putting on the necks of the disciples a yoke that neither we nor our fathers have been able to bear?" His point was that down through history the Jewish people had failed miserably in living up to the Law. Why then impose it on the Gentiles? Peter's words here are reminiscent of Jesus' words in Luke 11:46: "And you experts in the law, woe to you, because you load people down with burdens they can hardly carry, and you yourselves will not lift one finger to help them." The direction for the future needed to be one of grace. Sure, God still expected moral behavior from people. He was not eliminating the role of moral law (although Jesus simplified this law by saying it was summed up in essentially two commandments: love God with all your heart, mind, and soul; and love your neighbor as yourself). Rather, He was saying that legalism was a burden that no one needs to bear. Instead, we should love as He commanded, and then rely on God's grace and forgiveness when we fall short.

Who is it that seems to make the decision to not force circumcision?

When we look at the decision voiced in verse 19, it is interesting to note who actually decides. While some have seen Peter as "head" of the church at this point, it is James who actually makes the decision to not force circumcision. The rest of the church concurs, but the leadership seems to be James.

What four things does this Council ask Gentile converts not to do?

The Compromise

The essentials of the decision were that circumcision would not be required. However, they would ask Gentile converts to: (1) abstain from what has been sacrificed to idols, (2) abstain from blood, (3) abstain from what has been strangled, and (4) abstain from fornication. Why these particular restrictions? Basically this was a political compromise. They wanted to make sure that the Gentiles did not continue to do things that were part of their old idol worship, things that were abhorrent to what they had been taught as Jews. Eating strangled animals, or animals with the blood still in them, was against Jewish dietary law. Eating meat left over from a sacrifice to a foreign god was seen as participating in idol worship. Abstaining from fornication is the only true moral law that is mentioned. That is probably because in these times many of the foreign deities were fertility goddesses that were worshiped by going to a cult prostitute. Gentiles would have practiced this kind of "worship" many times before their conversion, and the Jewish leadership wanted to make sure that they truly turned away from it.

Did the decision of this First Church Council completely solve the conflict over circumcision? Support your answer.

While this council made a decision against requiring circumcision, it didn't entirely solve the problem between Gentile and Jewish Christians. In Paul's letter to the Galatians, written after these events, we see that the conflict persisted, and that even Peter vacillated on the issue (Gal. 2:11-14). However, in this decision the church had something to point to in mediating these conflicts and laying down a direction for the future. For the future of the church, this was a vital direction, because it made possible a much more open fellowship in which Gentiles could participate without cultural restraints.

notes:

Remain in groups of 6–8 people, in a horseshoe configuration.

In this small-group session, students will be applying the lessons of the text to their own lives through the following questions.

The students were asked (in the student book) to choose an answer for each question and explain why.

Learning from the Story (5-7 minutes)

1. What were the most important factors in solving this conflict? Rate each of the following factors from 1 (unimportant) to 5 (vital):

   ___ They openly expressed their opinions (vv. 1-2).
   ___ They appealed to respected authorities (v. 2).
   ___ They allowed much discussion rather than having one or two persons make a quick decision (v. 7).
   ___ They were sensitive to the Holy Spirit (vv. 8,12).

2. To what degree do you see what happened as a result of democratic deliberation; and to what degree do you see it as imposed by authorities? Mark the scale below:

   1 . . . . 2 . . . . 3 . . . . 4 5
   Democratic — Authoritarian

3. What implication does this incident have for the role of Old Testament law in the life of a Christian?

   ☐ It's all obsolete.
   ☐ Laws were kept or discarded by political compromise.
   ☐ The essential thing is faith in Christ—laws are secondary to that.
   ☐ God changed some laws that were unique to the Jews—all others remain.
   ☐ other: ____________________

notes:

life change lessons (5-7 minutes)

Share with the class the following thoughts on how the lessons of this text might be applied today. The answers to the student book questions (provided in the margin) are underlined unless the question requires a personal answer.

At first glance, a decision about circumcision may seem like it would have little relevance for the church today. If there is any conflict today about circumcision, it focuses on medical issues: Is there any real medical reason for it? Is it painful and even traumatic for the infant? Christians simply don't ask the question, "Is it important for my child's faith and salvation?"

What are some Old Testament laws and traditions that still cause debate among Christians today?

However, the relevance here has to do with resolving church conflicts, cultural inclusiveness, and knowing how to apply Old Testament laws and traditions to the Christian life. The issues of conflict resolution and cultural inclusiveness were dealt with in Sessions 4 and 6 of this study, respectively. The issue of applying Old Testament law and tradition is more complex. What about Old Testament dietary laws? Should we maintain the standards of Leviticus for sentencing in regard to crime and punishment? Is the Sabbath day (Saturday) still a day we should honor? Such questions remain complex, and on many of them different denominations would have decidedly different perspectives.

In acting on this session, then, what we need to do is get more in touch with our own church tradition and formulate our own position. Here are some suggestions on how to do this:

What are some specific issues we should discuss with our pastor?

1. INTERVIEW YOUR PASTOR OR OTHER INFLUENTIAL CHURCH TEACHER ON THE ROLE OF OLD TESTAMENT LAW AND TRADITION IN THE LIFE OF THE CHRISTIAN. Are some laws and traditions still to be observed, while some are not? How is it decided which laws still hold and which do not? Particularly, what does your tradition say about Sabbath observance and Old Testament dietary laws? How does your pastor see the decision in Acts 15 applying to the observance of such laws?

2. TALK WITH A FRIEND AND DISCOVER HIS UNDERSTANDING ON THE MATTER OF OLD TESTAMENT LAW. Why does he have a different position than your church?

3. WRITE OUT A STATEMENT OF YOUR OWN VIEW ON THE APPLICABILITY OF OLD TESTAMENT LAW FOR THE CHRISTIAN. Take into account what you learned in Steps 1 and 2. The statement should be as short and direct as possible, and it should help you differentiate between which Old Testament laws you should observe and which were only relevant to the culture of ancient Israel.

CARING TIME
Remain in groups of 6–8 people, in a horseshoe configuration.

Hand out the Prayer/Praise Report to the entire group. Ask each subgroup to pray for the empty chair. Pray specifically for God to guide you to someone to bring next week to fill that chair.

After a sufficient time of prayer in subgroups, close in a corporate prayer. Say, "Next week we will talk about: 'A Spirit-Led Journey.' "

Remind participants of the daily Scripture readings and reflective questions found on page 89.

Caring Time (15-20 minutes)

Use this time to pray for one another. Begin by having each group member answer the following question:

"With what conflict (internal or interpersonal) could you use prayer support right now?"

Then pray for these conflicts. Remember to use the Prayer/Praise Report and pray for the requests and concerns listed.

notes:

Reference Notes

Use these notes to gain further understanding of the text as you study on your own:

BIBLE STUDY NOTES

ACTS 15:1–35
church council

Right in the middle of Luke's account is this record of the council in Jerusalem that met to discuss the status of Gentiles in the church. This critical meeting of the church marked its first self-conscious departure from orthodox Judaism. Had the council decided to support the claims of the Jewish believers, Christianity would have remained only another sect within Judaism.

ACTS 15:1–4
controversy

The controversy surrounding circumcision stirred up such a debate that the church felt it necessary to call together the recognized leaders from Jerusalem and Antioch to settle the issue. This is considered to be the First Church Council.

ACTS 15:5
resistance

the believers who belonged to the party of the Pharisees. The resistance to allowing Gentiles into the church originated with Jewish Christians who had formerly been Pharisees. This small but influential sect was widely respected for its adherence to the Law and traditions. Their concern arose from a genuine desire to insure that God's honor was not violated through disregard of His Law. To them, the offer of the gospel apart from the Law was inconceivable since for centuries their people had been taught to look to the Law to discern God's will. Paul's ministry seemed like a slap in Israel's face—an unthinkable rejection of all the covenant responsibilities of God's chosen people.

ACTS 15:7–8
acceptance

As part of the discussion, Peter recounts his experience with Cornelius, which may have occurred ten or more years earlier (Acts 10:1–11:18). The fact that Cornelius experienced the presence of the Spirit in the same way the disciples did was proof to him that God accepted the Gentiles quite apart from the practice of Jewish law.

ACTS 15:9–11
purity

It is by faith in Jesus that one is made pure by God. The fact that it has to be that way is made plain by the fact that neither Israel as a nation nor any Jew as an individual ever managed to live up to all the demands of the Law. This affirmation of God's intent to save Gentiles through faith in Jesus is Peter's last statement in Acts.

ACTS 15:13–21
God's plan

James was the leader of the Jerusalem church, and the ultimate decision as to the position of the Jerusalem church was his to make. Since in Galatians 2:11–13 James appears to have represented those who believed that Gentiles could not be considered equal members of the church with Jews, it may be that this council was the turning point when he realized the scope of Jesus' mission. James' affirmation of God's plan to save all types of people through faith in Jesus is his last statement in Acts as well.

ACTS 15:15
truth

the words of the prophets. James' quote is primarily rooted in the Septuagint version of Amos 9:11–12. The Old Testament books of Hosea through Malachi were contained on a single scroll. To quote one was to assume the support of the others.

ACTS 15:16–18
anticipation

The original context of the prophecy was the anticipation of the destruction of Israel (722 B.C.) after which God would one day return the nation to its former glory as in David's day. James sees that the way God is rebuilding "David's ... tent" (a symbol of God's presence with Israel) is by establishing His church, made up of all types of people who seek God. The differences between the Septuagint version quoted here and what is found in our Old Testament are a result of adding a *d* to the Hebrew word *yiresu* (possessing) to obtain *yirdresu* (seeking), and a dispute about whether the Hebrew word *dm* should be vocalized as *Edom* (the name of a country south of Israel) or as *adam* (the Hebrew word for humanity). In either case, the point is that God's new people will include Gentiles as well as Jews.

ACTS 15:20
obedience

telling them to abstain. These considerations sum up the Law in Leviticus 17–27 that applied to Israel and all foreigners who lived within her borders.
food polluted by idols. In Gentile areas meat was sold only after the animal had been sacrificed as part of a worship service to an idol. The eating of such food was later to be a source of controversy between Jewish and Gentile believers in Rome (Rom. 14:1-8) and Corinth (1 Cor. 8).
sexual immorality. This may be related to "the pollution of idols" since idolatry sometimes involved ritual prostitution (1 Cor. 6:12-20).
meat of strangled animals and from blood. Jews were forbidden to eat meat that had any blood in it (Lev. 17:10-14). Gentiles would make the sharing of meals with Jewish believers easier if they would respect this tradition.

Session

10

A Spirit-Led Journey

Prepare for the Session

	READINGS	REFLECTIVE QUESTIONS
Monday	Acts 16:6–10	Who is God calling you to help right now? In what ways can you be of help to this person?
Tuesday	Acts 16:11–15	Do you have the gift of hospitality? If so, in what ways can you use it more to the glory of God?
Wednesday	Acts 16:25–31	What brought you to a realization that you needed to be saved? Take time to praise God for His grace.
Thursday	Acts 16:32–34	Do you still have the joy you first felt when you came to Christ? If so, how are you expressing that joy? If not, how can joy be restored to your life?
Friday	Acts 17:1–4	Are you maintaining a habit of regular worship? Are you an active part of what happens, or are you just an observer?
Saturday	Acts 17:5–9	Do you try to "not make waves," or are you willing to "rock the boat" when it is necessary?
Sunday	Acts 17:10–12	Are you examining the Scriptures regularly? If so, how is that discipline changing you?

notes:

OUR GOALS FOR THIS SESSION ARE:

BIBLE STUDY	• to appreciate the role of the Holy Spirit in directing Paul's path in his mission work • to see how Christian faith first came to Europe • to consider how the Holy Spirit's guidance can be discerned
LIFE CHANGE	• to provide for a "life direction evaluation period" during the coming week • to begin each day with prayer • to not overload our agenda

In groups of 6–8, gather people in a horseshoe configuration.

Make sure everyone has a name tag.

Take time to share information on class parties that are coming up as well as any relevant church events.

INTRODUCE THE ICEBREAKER ACTIVITY: The students have been told in their books to choose one answer.

After the Icebreaker, say something like, "Whatever our travel plans are, most of us know that they are sometimes changed by circumstances. That is essentially what happened with Paul's second missionary journey, when God redirected him to a new destination. This change in itinerary greatly changed the course of history. Let's look at how it happened."

Hand out the Prayer/Praise Report. A sample copy is on pages 158-159. Have people write down prayer requests and praises. Then have the prayer coordinator collect the report and make copies for use during the Caring Time.

Icebreaker (10-15 minutes)

Travel Plans. Go around the group on question 1, letting everyone share. Then do the same with questions 2 and 3.

1. If you could travel to any country in the world for a visit, where would you want to go?

2. Who, besides immediate family, would you choose as traveling companions?

3. If money were no object, which of the following would be your preferred mode of travel?

- ☐ private jet
- ☐ a private yacht
- ☐ a chauffeur-driven limo
- ☐ a luxury cruise liner
- ☐ a train with a private berth
- ☐ a luxury RV, with all the conveniences of home

10

notes:

LEARNING FROM THE BIBLE

ACTS 16:6-15

Have a member of the class, selected ahead of time, read the passage from Acts.

Bible Study (30-45 minutes)

The Scripture for this week:

*[6]Paul and his companions traveled throughout the region of
Phrygia and Galatia, having been kept by the Holy Spirit from
preaching the word in the province of Asia. [7]When they came to the
border of Mysia, they tried to enter Bithynia, but the Spirit of Jesus
would not allow them to. [8]So they passed by Mysia and went down
to Troas. [9]During the night Paul had a vision of a man of Macedonia
standing and begging him, "Come over to Macedonia and help us."
[10]After Paul had seen the vision, we got ready at once to leave for
Macedonia, concluding that God had called us to preach the gospel
to them.*

*[11]From Troas we put out to sea and sailed straight for Samothrace,
and the next day on the Neapolis. [12]From there we traveled to Philippi,
a Roman colony and the leading city of that district of Macedonia.
And we stayed there several days.*

*[13]On the Sabbath we went outside the city gate to the river, where
we expected to find a place of prayer. We sat down and began to
speak to the women who had gathered there. [14]One of those listening
was a woman named Lydia, a dealer in purple cloth from the city of
Thyatira, who was a worshiper of God. The Lord opened her heart to
respond to Paul's message. [15]When she and the members of her
household were baptized, she invited us to her home. "If you consider me a believer in the Lord," she said, "come and stay at my house."
And she persuaded us.*

notes:

Summarize these introductory remarks. Be sure to include the underlined information, which gives the answers to the student book questions (provided in the margin).

What poet is mentioned as one who chose between two diverging paths? What basis did this person use for making his choice of path?

How did Paul's method of choosing which path to take differ from the poet's?

...about today's session (5 minutes)

THE HOLY SPIRIT'S GUIDANCE

Poet Robert Frost wrote a much-loved poem about "two roads that diverged in a yellow wood," and the difficulty he had in choosing which one to take. There seemed at first no way to differentiate between the two choices, but finally he decided to take "the one less traveled-by." For him, that choice made all the difference. Well, the Apostle Paul also came to such a divergence of roads where he had to decide which one to take. His criterion for decision-making was different than Frost's, however. He chose the road that the Spirit directed him to take. The results were virtually the same as for Frost—the road he took made all the difference. The Spirit led him to head into Europe, and the Christian Church became established on the continent from which it spread throughout the world.

When we look back on such events, it's easy to look upon them as unique. The Holy Spirit acted in a unique way with a unique human being, the Apostle Paul. However, God still has much that He wants to do in the world—there are many people He wants to hear the gospel and many people to whom He wants to show His love. Isn't it reasonable that the Holy Spirit would still guide those who are seeking to be part of such work of God? Besides being reasonable, it is also part of the promises of our Lord, who told us that we would do great things through the Holy Spirit (John 14:12,25-26). What we need to do, then, is to have the same sensitivity to the Spirit's guidance that Paul had. That is what we will seek to learn more about in this session.

notes:

Remain in groups of 6–8 people, in a horseshoe configuration.

In this small-group session, students will be responding to the following questions that will help them share their stories in terms of Paul's trip to Macedonia.

Have the students explore these questions together.

Identifying with the Story (5-7 minutes)

1. When have unforeseen obstacles necessitated a change in plans for you?

2. How do you generally react when you have to make a change in plans (a long-planned vacation is delayed, rain cancels the picnic, etc.)?

   - ☐ "Que sera, sera!"
   - ☐ A little irritated, but able to adapt.
   - ☐ A total "basket-case"!
   - ☐ Really upset for a while.

3. When has a change in plans brought an unexpected "serendipity" into your life?

notes:

today's session (15-20 minutes)

Share with your class the following information which you may modify according to your own perspectives and teaching needs. The answers to the student book questions (provided in the margin) are underlined.

Name at least three important actions of the Holy Spirit in Acts:

One of the most obvious facts about the work of the church in Acts is that the Holy Spirit was an integral part of all that happened. The Holy Spirit is referred to no less than 41 times in the book. First, the Holy Spirit filled the disciples at Pentecost (Acts 2). The Holy Spirit also helped Peter when he was hauled before the Sanhedrin (4:8); filled Stephen in his hour of martyrdom (7:55); healed Saul's (Paul's) blindness (9:17-19); brought increased numbers to the church (9:31); led Gentiles to become believers (10:44-48); set apart Paul and Barnabas for their missionary journeys (13:2); and prepared Paul for the suffering he would face (20:23).

Paul's Sensitivity to the Holy Spirit

In our passage for this week, the Apostle Paul shows a special sensitivity to the Holy Spirit's leading, and as a result he is led to take the gospel to Europe for the first time. How significant this is! It was in Europe that the gospel grew and was spread throughout the rest of the earth. Because it became the dominant faith in Europe, it came to America and became the dominant faith here as well. Let's look at this story more closely in order to understand what it says to us about this important milestone in church history, as well as what it says to us today.

In what town in the province of Asia did Paul later have a very successful mission?

The events of this chapter occur in what is called Paul's second missionary journey. A particularly striking phrase is found in verse 6, "having been kept by the Holy Spirit from preaching the word in the province of Asia." It's important to note that this is not the continent we think of when we think of Asia, but rather the Roman province of Asia. This is in present-day Turkey. What did it mean that Paul was "kept by the Holy Spirit" from preaching in Asia? We don't really know exactly how this message was conveyed to Paul and his missionary team. But the way it is phrased it seems more than simply sensing it might not be a good idea. They had a strong conviction that the Holy Spirit did not want them to go in that direction. Why not? Perhaps it was because of the strength of the Jewish opposition in that area. Perhaps it was that the time was not right in Asia yet. Paul would later spend three years at Ephesus, which was part of this region, and his ministry would be very successful (Acts 19:1-41). It may have been so successful because Paul had waited for the Holy Spirit to show him the time was right. It is also possible that the Holy Spirit was saying that getting the gospel to Europe was so crucial it had to be done right away.

today's session (cont'd)

What events may Paul have interpreted as meaning that the Holy Spirit or Spirit of Christ did not want him going into Asia or Bithynia? What vision redirected his path?

A second prohibition by the Holy Spirit came when Paul tried to go into the region of Bithynia. This was a province to the north of where they were. In essence, they were told not to divert their path to the right or the left, but go straight ahead, which would have been the direction of Europe. When they got to Troas, which is on the Aegean Sea across from Greece, Paul saw a vision at night. It was a man of Macedonia, calling them "to come over and help us." Macedonia is part of Greece. Right away Paul knew that this was why they had been forbidden to go in the directions he had considered. He did not hesitate to follow what he believed to be the call of the Holy Spirit. Our text tells us "we got ready at once to leave for Macedonia" (v. 10).

Luke Joins the Team

What do scholars believe is the significance of the change from "they" to "we" in the narrative of Acts?

There is another significance to what is said in verse 10. Previously, our text referred to Paul and his group as "they." In verse 10, we find this changing to "we." Scholars generally agree this means that Luke, the author of Acts, joined the missionary team at this point. Luke was a Gentile physician. Was he converted at this point? While there is no evidence that Luke was converted through Paul's ministry, this was the first time the gospel had come this far west. In any case, he was without doubt thrilled that the Holy Spirit had seen fit to redirect Paul from going to Asia and Bithynia.

Paul and his group crossed into Macedonia and settled in Philippi, the principal city of the region. Paul's later letter to the Philippians is one of his warmest, most positive letters, and it indicates that the church here was very supportive of him, even when other churches seemed to have forgotten about his needs (Phil. 4:15-16).

The First Convert in Europe

Who seems to have been the first convert in Europe?

The first person who is named as a convert to Christ in Europe was a woman—Lydia of Thyatira. She was a dealer in purple cloth. The city of Thyatira was famous for its trade in purple dyes. These dyes were made by taking the glands of the myrax, a purple sea snail, and simmering them in pans for a few days. They then dipped cloth in it for a dye that would never fade. This purple was considered a royal color, and there were laws in Rome that limited who could wear it. But obviously, selling such a luxurious cloth meant that Lydia was a wealthy woman. Being part of a Greek culture meant that she had more opportunities to be involved in a business like this than did Hebrew women. However, she was also what was referred to as "a worshiper of God." That meant that, while a Gentile, she worshiped the God of Abraham. She was not a full proselyte, possibly because she did not want to be bound by Jewish ceremo-

What business did this convert have, and why was it particularly lucrative?

nial law. Her status in this regard was very much like Cornelius, the centurion we studied a few sessions ago. She was probably not married (perhaps divorced or widowed), since the text refers to "her household." Had a husband been around it would have been referred to as "his household" and Lydia could not have made a decision regarding their baptism, as it at least appears she did here. Lydia's home became their base of operations while in the region (16:15,40).

So then, as a result of following the guidance of the Holy Spirit Luke joined the missionary team; who became a valued missionary companion, authored two books of the Bible; a wealthy woman was converted who became a valuable supporter of Christ; and a church was started that became one of Paul's most loyal churches. What better commendation could there be for following the guidance of the Spirit?

notes:

Remain in groups of 6–8 people, in a horseshoe configuration.

In this small-group session, students will be applying the lessons of the text to their own lives through the following questions.

The students were asked (in the student book) to choose an answer for each question and explain why.

Learning from the Story (5-7 minutes)

1. Why did Paul have such a strong sense of the Holy Spirit's guidance?

   - ▢ He was Paul, a saint—God spoke more directly to him.
   - ▢ It was one of his gifts—like being a psychic.
   - ▢ He prayed for the Spirit's guidance, and kept open to that guidance.
   - ▢ He didn't—it was just his way of interpreting coincidences.
   - ▢ other: ________________________________

2. Had Paul *not* been sensitive to the Spirit's guidance, how would it have affected the conversion of Lydia in particular and Europe in general? Would God have just found another way?

3. What obstacles do you see ahead of you in your present life path? Are these obstacles just normal obstacles that come to life, or are these obstacles God's way of telling you to take another direction? How can you tell?

notes:

Share with the class the following thoughts on how the lessons of this text might be applied today. The answers to the student book questions (provided in the margin) are underlined unless the question requires a personal answer.

How does rushing around make it difficult for you to be in touch with the Holy Spirit?

Why is it sometimes difficult to evaluate what it means when you encounter obstacles in the way of your goals?

life change lessons (5-7 minutes)

At first glance, when we think about what we should *do* in response to today's lesson, we may be a little mystified. Certainly we can't plan to have a dream that will redirect where we go for the weeks to come. We can do several other things, however. One is to keep ourselves open to the direction of the Spirit, however the direction of the Spirit may come to us. This calls for slowing down enough to pay attention to such direction. <u>When we are rushing around a step or two behind on our overly full agenda</u>, <u>we seldom have the sensitivity to be in touch with the Holy Spirit</u>. A second thing we need to do is learn to evaluate the obstacles that come into our life. Most likely, it was such obstacles that conveyed to Paul that the Spirit did not want him to go to Asia and Bithynia. Evaluating such obstacles is not easy. <u>Do they mean that we just need to try harder, believing the obstacles are there to test our resolve</u>? <u>Or do they mean we need to consider another direction</u>, <u>as Paul did</u>?

What we have been talking about is a change of attitude. However, to be most helpful, we need to look beyond these general attitudinal issues to specific behaviors that will help us make the needed behavior changes. Here are some suggestions:

1. PROVIDE FOR A "LIFE DIRECTION EVALUATION PERIOD" DURING THE COMING WEEK. Set aside at least an hour to consider where you are going in life. Where do you see yourself in one year? In five years? Is there a tension between where you would like to be going, and where you believe the Holy Spirit is leading you? What obstacles are you confronting, and what might they mean? Include some time for scriptural study and prayer in this evaluation time.

2. BEGIN EACH DAY WITH PRAYER. In this prayer time, seek God's direction for that day. Don't just talk to God, but listen as well. Take time to consider where the Holy Spirit might be leading you in your day.

3. DON'T OVERLOAD YOUR AGENDA. Rushing around keeps a person from really thinking about what they are doing or being sensitive to the moment. All you can think about is "I'm not getting done what I planned to get done." Then often you don't see what God's agenda is for you for that day. Perhaps God is trying to lead you to that one activity or relationship that will make the entire day, or even your entire week or month, meaningful.

CARING TIME
Remain in groups of 6–8 people, in a horseshoe configuration.

Hand out the Prayer/Praise Report to the entire group. Ask each subgroup to pray for the empty chair. Pray specifically for God to guide you to someone to bring next week to fill that chair.

After a sufficient time of prayer in subgroups, close in a corporate prayer. Say, "Next week we will talk about: 'Speaking the Language of the Culture.' "

Remind participants of the daily Scripture readings and reflective questions found on page 97.

Caring Time (15-20 minutes)

Close by sharing prayer requests and praying for one another. Begin by having each member of the group finish the sentence:

"Right now I am seeking the guidance of the Holy Spirit to ..."

Then pray for these needs for guidance. In addition, pray for the concerns on the Prayer/Praise Report.

notes:

BIBLE STUDY NOTES

Reference Notes

Use these notes to gain further understanding of the text as you study on your own:

ACTS 16:6–7
guidance

the Holy Spirit ... the Spirit of Jesus. Luke clearly identifies the ongoing work of Jesus with the agency of the Holy Spirit in the lives of the apostles.

ACTS 16:7

would not allow them to. Why Jesus would not allow Paul and Silas to preach in Asia and Bithyna is not given. Later on, the Apostle Peter was in contact with churches in that area so they were not left bereft of the gospel (1 Peter 1:1).

ACTS 16:8

Troas. An important seaport on the Aegean Sea. While it appears Paul did not do any evangelistic work here at this time, he did do so later on (2 Cor. 2:12).

ACTS 16:9
northern Greece

Macedonia. This area of northern Greece had been the dominant power under Alexander the Great in the fourth century B.C.

ACTS 16:10

we. Verses 10–17 is the first of the passages written in the first person (20:5–21:18; 27:1–28:16), indicating that Luke himself was accompanying Paul at these points.

ACTS 16:11–12
Roman province

In two days they arrived at Macedonia, landing at Neapolis. Philippi was a short distance to the west.

ACTS 16:12

the leading city of that district. The Greek here is uncertain. Since Philippi was neither the largest city nor the capital of the province, it probably should read simply, "a city of the first district of Macedonia." Macedonia was a Roman province divided into four districts.

ACTS 16:13
worship

Ten men were required in order to form a synagogue. The fact that there was no synagogue in Philippi indicates how small the Jewish population was.
outside the city gate to the river. The Jews may have been forbidden to meet inside the city limits, or they may have wanted to be near a river to perform their ceremonial washings.

ACTS 16:14
faith

Lydia. Macedonian women enjoyed far more freedom and opportunities than many of their counterparts elsewhere. Lydia was a businesswoman involved in selling purple cloth, a luxury item indicating that she was a woman of wealth.
Thyatira. A city in the province of Asia noted for its dyeing industry. Evidence indicates that there was a Jewish community in Thyatira, which probably influenced Lydia toward faith in the God of the Jews. Lydia demonstrated her faith in Jesus as the Messiah by baptism and by offering hospitality to the missionaries.

ACTS 16:15

the members of her household. It was customary for children and servants to embrace the faith of their master or mistress (Acts 11:14).

notes:

Session 11

Speaking the Language of the Culture

Prepare for the Session

	READINGS	REFLECTIVE QUESTIONS
Monday	Acts 17:16–21	What is distressing you the most about the society in which you are living? How well are you dealing with that stress?
Tuesday	Acts 17:22–28	In what ways might you be subjecting God to human limitations? What would it mean for you to expand your vision of Him?
Wednesday	Acts 17:29–34	How well do you handle the cynicism of others concerning the beliefs you hold dear?
Thursday	Acts 18:9–11	To what degree are you allowing fear to keep you from speaking up for your faith?
Friday	Acts 18:18–22	How much do you let God help you plan your itinerary as you go from place to place in your life?
Saturday	Acts 18:23–26	How receptive to correction are you? If God wanted to speak through some one else to change a misconception you have, would you be willing to listen?
Sunday	Acts 18:27–28	How is God using you right now to help other believers?

notes:

OUR GOALS FOR THIS SESSION ARE:

In groups of 6–8, gather people in a horseshoe configuration.

Make sure everyone has a name tag.

Take time to share information on class parties that are coming up as well as any relevant church events.

INTRODUCE THE ICEBREAKER ACTIVITY: The students have been told in their books to choose one answer.

After the Icebreaker, say something like, "Perhaps because of the startlingly new nature of his message, some people thought Paul was crazy. But time has proven the opposite to be true—Paul was one of the clearest thinkers of his time. In our session this week we will look at how his message was received in the intellectual center of his day—Athens."

Hand out the Prayer/Praise Report. A sample copy is on pages 158-159. Have people write down prayer requests and praises. Then have the prayer coordinator collect the report and make copies for use during the Caring Time.

BIBLE STUDY
- to evaluate Paul's message and evangelistic method in Athens
- to consider how to keep gospel truth, while adapting methods to speak to different cultures
- to learn how to challenge the "gods" of a culture

LIFE CHANGE
- to discover one song of youth culture that proclaims a positive value
- to find a distinctive subculture in our town and learn what this subculture values
- to discover how our worship services can speak to the youth culture

Icebreaker (10-15 minutes)

My Sanity Defense. Go around the group on question 1 and have everyone answer. Then go around again on question 2.

1. If someone were to put you on trial to accuse you of not being sane, to what evidence would they likely point?

   - ☐ I have volunteered to chaperone teenagers.
   - ☐ I volunteered to teach my teenager how to drive.
   - ☐ I once walked between a group of men and a TV when they were watching the Super Bowl.
   - ☐ I have driven a car in Europe.
   - ☐ I once invited my in-laws to live with us for a while.
   - ☐ other: ______________________________

2. Which of the following songs best describe what you would anticipate the outcome of the trial to be? (Put an "X" on the continuum to show which you would be closest to.)

"You may be right;
I may be crazy?"
(Billy Joel) .... "I'm All Right" (Kenny Loggins)

notes:

LEARNING FROM THE BIBLE

ACTS 17:16-34

Have four members of the class, selected ahead of time, read the passage from Acts. Have one member read the narration, one member read the part of Paul (vv. 22b-31), and two members read the part of those who reacted to Paul (vv. 18-20,32b).

Bible Study (30-45 minutes)

The Scripture for this week:

*16While Paul was waiting for them in Athens, he was greatly dis-
tressed to see that the city was full of idols. 17So he reasoned in the
synagogue with the Jews and the God-fearing Greeks, as well as in
the marketplace day by day with those who happened to be there. 18A
group of Epicurean and Stoic philosophers began to dispute with
him. Some of them asked, "What is this babbler trying to say?"
Others remarked, "He seems to be advocating foreign gods." They
said this because Paul was preaching the good news about Jesus and
the resurrection. 19Then they took him and brought him to a meeting
of the Areopagus, where they said to him, "May we know what this
new teaching is that you are presenting? 20You are bringing some
strange ideas to our ears, and we want to know what they mean."
21(All the Athenians and the foreigners who lived there spent their
time doing nothing but talking about and listening to the latest ideas.)*

*22Paul then stood up in the meeting of the Areopogus and said:
"Men of Athens! I see that in every way you are very religious. 23For as
I walked around and looked carefully at your objects of worship, I even
found an altar with this inscription: TO AN UNKNOWN GOD. Now what
you worship as something unknown I am going to proclaim to you.*

*24"The God who made the world and everything in it is the Lord
of heaven and earth and does not live in temples built by hands.
25And he is not served by human hands, as if he needed anything,
because he himself gives all men life and breath and everything else.
26From one man he made every nation of men, that they should
inhabit the whole earth; and he determined the times set for them and
the exact places where they should live. 27God did this so that men
would seek him and perhaps reach out for him and find him, though he
is not far from each one of us. 28'For in him we live and move and have
our being.' As some of your own poets have said, 'We are his offspring.'*

*29"Therefore since we are God's offspring, we should not think
that the divine being is like gold or silver or stone—an image made
by man's design and skill. 30In the past God overlooked such ignorance, but now he commands all people everywhere to repent. 31For
he has set a day when he will judge the world with justice by the man
he has appointed. He has given proof of this to all men by raising
him from the dead."*

*32When they heard about the resurrection of the dead, some of
them sneered, but others said, "We want to hear you again on this*

> subject." 33At that, Paul left the Council. 34A few men became followers of Paul and believed. Among them was Dionysius, a member of the Areopagus, also a woman named Damaris, and a number of others.

notes:

Summarize these introductory remarks. Be sure to include the underlined information, which gives the answers to the student book questions (provided in the margin).

What are some cultural changes that have occurred since 1950?

...about today's session (5 minutes)

SPEAKING TO TODAY'S CULTURE

In North America we live in a culture that has changed appreciably in the last 50 years. Rock 'n' roll music, and its many variants, has dominated the music scene for younger people, and has been part of a rift between those born in the rock era and those born before it all started. The dominant culture that was heavily influenced by rural life and values before 1950 has increasingly become urbanized, and fewer and fewer people have any direct acquaintance with what rural life is about. Religious teaching and values, which were taught in the schools and were part of the culture in the early to middle part of the twentieth century, have been pushed to the side by a variety of Supreme Court rulings. And the meaning of "community" has changed as people seem to talk less and less with those in their own neighborhoods, but communicate more and more with people around the world via the Internet.

In the midst of all of these changes, many older church leaders look back wistfully and wish their church could be like it was in the 1950s—packed worship services and Sunday schools full of young people. But can the church speak to a 21st-century culture, if it still speaks in the language of the 1950s? Can the church take the gospel that has been around for 2000 years and effectively put it in the language of a changing culture? As Rick Warren of the Saddleback

...about today's session (cont'd)

What extremes does Rick Warren say different churches go to in relation to the culture?

Community Church writes, "On the one hand we are obligated to remain faithful to the unchanging Word of God. On the other hand, we must minister in an ever-changing world. Sadly, many Christians unwilling to live with this tension retreat to one of two extremes. ... Some churches, fearing worldly infection, retreat into isolation from today's culture. ... Then there are those who, fearing irrelevance, foolishly imitate the latest fad and fashion."[1] Can the church speak to today's culture while retaining the unchanging Word of God?

When Paul went to Athens, he took on the challenge of putting the gospel into the language of another culture. How did he do this, and what can we learn as we speak to what seems like a "foreign" culture on our own soil? That is what this session will be about.

notes:

Remain in groups of 6–8 people, in a horseshoe configuration.

In this small-group session, students will be responding to the following questions that will help them share their stories in terms of Paul's interaction with the Athenians.

Have the students explore these questions together.

Identifying with the Story (5-7 minutes)

1. When you were in school, who were you most likely to get into an argument with?

- ☐ my brother or sister
- ☐ my father
- ☐ my mother
- ☐ other: ________________
- ☐ kids of the opposite sex
- ☐ my friends
- ☐ nobody—I never argued.

2. Where was the place you and your friends most frequently gathered to talk things over?

- ☐ a local soda fountain or drive-in
- ☐ a school playground
- ☐ the swimming pool
- ☐ a neighborhood park
- ☐ a friend's house
- ☐ We just talked on the phone.

3. In the town or city you grew up in, what would you say were the "gods" of the town?

   - ☐ Sports—They worshiped the local _________ team.
   - ☐ Money—They would do anything for a buck.
   - ☐ Sex—It was a regular Peyton Place.
   - ☐ The Status Quo—Anyone challenging it was exiled.
   - ☐ The Perfect Lawn—Anyone stepping on one had violated "Holy Ground."
   - ☐ other: ______________________________

notes:

Share with your class the following information which you may modify according to your own perspectives and teaching needs. The answers to the student book questions (provided in the margin) are underlined.

today's session (15-20 minutes)

Christianity has always clashed in one way or another with the culture in which it has found itself. Jesus spoke of this in an indirect way when he said in John 15:19, "If you belonged to the world, it would love you as its own. As it is, you do not belong to the world, but I have chosen you out of the world. That is why the world hates you." "Hates" may be a stronger word than is true for most Christians. Jesus often taught by the use of hyperbole. However, most Christians do at one time or another feel the pinch of being in conflict with the values and direction of the secular society in which they live. When we feel this way, how do we react? Looking at how the Apostle Paul reacted when he felt like "a fish out of water" in the culture of Athens may help us in our consideration of this issue. We will consider how Paul reacted in four different ways to this cultural dilemma.

today's session (cont'd)

The Reaction of Shock

What "greatly distressed" Paul when he was in Athens?

When Paul encountered for himself what was happening in Athens, his first reaction was one of shock. Verse 16 tells us, "While Paul was waiting for them in Athens, he was greatly distressed to see that the city was full of idols." Those of you who are familiar with what the Greek culture of Athens was like might ask Paul, "What did you expect? Didn't you know that this was what you would find in Athens?" No doubt Paul did understand what Athens would be like. However, there is a difference between knowing something in your mind and then actually confronting it face-to-face. We all "know" that one day we are going to die. But this is not the same as when the doctor tells us that we only have a few months to live. The difference is emotional impact. The distress that Paul experienced in Athens was due to the emotional impact of what he had previously known to be true—Athens was a city that worshiped many false gods.

What are some examples of things Christians find shocking today?

Christians today can also be shocked by some of the things that happen in our culture. Secular artists depict Christ or something we deem as holy in an unholy way. Pornography of all kinds and degrees of offensiveness is pushed over the Internet, and many defend it under the guise of freedom of speech. Neo-Nazis seek to deny the Holocaust and refer to Christ in justifying their racial hatred. There are things Christians are rightfully shocked about in today's world.

But should shock be our only reaction? We note that some people and groups even seek to shock Christians. They enjoy seeing the reaction of shock from people of faith. It reinforces their image of themselves as independent rebels. In some respects being shocked just plays into their hands. If we want to change people we need to go beyond a reaction of shock to a more proactive approach, just as the Apostle Paul did.

Affirming What Is Good

How did Paul use affirmation in his ministry?

After his initial shock, Paul turned to a more positive reaction of affirming what was good. He told the Athenians, "I see that in every way you are very religious" (v. 22). He could have said, "I see that you are all superstitious idolaters," but he knew that a positive approach was what changes people. He used the same positive approach in most of his letters, where he almost always began by affirming what the believers were doing right. The church at Corinth was being torn apart by divisiveness, but Paul started off his first letter by referring to the grace given to them (1 Cor. 1:4), along with spiritual gifts (1 Cor. 1:7). Some members of the church at Thessalonica were lax in their sexual morals and others were lazy,

Why is affirmation important in helping people to change?

but he started off his letter to them affirming how they imitated the Lord (1 Thess. 1:6), and how they were a model to other believers (1 Thess. 1:7). Affirmation helps keep people from getting discouraged in their quest to do better, and it shows that you are not just looking to be a critical person.

Speaking in the Language of the Culture

When in Athens, why did Paul refer to the sayings of Greek poets instead of quoting Old Testament prophecy?

A second thing that Paul did was that he spoke to the Athenians in the language of their culture. He referred to their statue "TO AN UNKNOWN GOD" (v. 23) and to the teachings of their poets (v. 28). This helped the people know that Paul knew and respected the contributions of their culture. What Paul didn't do was talk to them about all the prophecies of Hebrew Scripture. It wouldn't have made sense to them and they wouldn't have respected the source of authority. And so when the church speaks to the younger generation today, the church shouldn't just refer to the thinkers and songs of previous generations. We speak best when we affirm the positive messages that can be found in some of the music and movies of the young, and not just put them down for the negative messages.

Remaining Focused on the Message

Paul knew that apart from ______________ ______________ this new faith would have no reason for existence and would have nothing to say to anyone.

While Paul adapted the form of his message to the culture of Athens, he did not compromise the message itself. While he undoubtedly knew that the philosophers of Athens would be skeptical of any teaching about resurrection, he proclaimed it boldly (vv. 31-32). He knew that apart from the resurrection of Jesus Christ, this new faith would have no reason for existence, and would have nothing to say to anyone (1 Cor. 15:12-28). Some advocate changing the message of Christianity—soft-pedaling the cross or spiritualizing the resurrection—in order to make it supposedly more palatable to the modern world. But that is not what Paul did. He later wrote to the Corinthians, "... we preach Christ crucified: a stumbling block to Jews and foolishness to Gentiles, but to those whom God has called, both Jews and Greeks, Christ the power of God and the wisdom of God" (1 Cor. 1:23-24).

Others advocate not challenging people's erroneous conceptions and their "false gods." But Paul was bold to tell the Athenians that their approach to God was misguided—they needed to turn from gods made by people who lived in temples made by people to the Creator of the Universe (vv. 24-29). We should not compromise our message either. Rather, we need to have enough confidence in its truth to believe that if we show some sensitivity to the culture of the recipients, the truth will strike home and we will be able to be used by God to convert some modern equivalents to Dionysius and Damaris.

Remain in groups of 6–8 people, in a horseshoe configuration.

In this small-group session, students will be applying the lessons of the text to their own lives through the following questions.

The students were asked (in the student book) to choose an answer for each question and explain why.

Learning from the Story (5-7 minutes)

1. What surprises you the most in this story?
   - ☐ That a sophisticated traveler like Paul would be shocked by the idols of Athens.
   - ☐ That the idol-worshiping Greeks seemed to listen to Paul better than the Jews did.
   - ☐ That Paul knew and quoted Greek poets.
   - ☐ That people then scoffed at the idea of a resurrection.
   - ☐ That Paul made converts even in a sophisticated audience such as this.
   - ☐ other:__________________________________

2. What do you think convinced these Athenians to give Paul a chance to speak in the Areopagus?
   - ☐ his eloquence
   - ☐ the power and influence of the Holy Spirit
   - ☐ their curiosity
   - ☐ their hunger for the answers Paul was giving them
   - ☐ other:__________________________________

3. What do you think was the most effective thing Paul did in Athens?
   - ☐ He affirmed their religious inclinations.
   - ☐ He referred to the poets and thinkers of Greece.
   - ☐ He showed the fallacy of worshiping gods made by hands.
   - ☐ He boldly proclaimed the resurrection to those who were skeptical about it.
   - ☐ other:__________________________________

notes:

life change lessons (5-7 minutes)

Share with the class the following thoughts on how the lessons of this text might be applied today. The answers to the student book questions (provided in the margin) are underlined unless the question requires a personal answer.

A Christian who really wants to be part of changing people's lives for Jesus Christ cannot afford to be ethnocentric. There are too many cultures in our world for us to ignore them and focus only on our own. When we do so the Christian faith begins to look like a localized cult that proclaims a "tribal god" who is only interested in certain people. But we worship the God who is the Creator and the Redeemer of the Universe! What is true for the individual Christian is even more true for the church that seeks to reach out.

What are some examples of cultures to which we need to reach out?

In order to make this change, we need first of all to broaden our cultural awareness. The culture of the young was mentioned earlier. Some people have a natural connection to that culture–they are young themselves or they have teenage or young adult children. Others, however, may have to go out of their way to talk to young people to gain a greater awareness of their culture. But the culture of the young is not the only culture the church needs to reach out to: there are a growing variety of ethnic cultures in our country as well as occupational subcultures (farmers, oil workers, fishermen, the military, etc.) and lifestyle subcultures (motorcyclists, computer hackers, the homeless, etc.) To reach out to persons of each group it will help us to know something of what their culture is like, and to respect that culture.

Here are some suggestions of what this might mean in terms of practical actions:

With what expressions of youth culture are we encouraged to familiarize ourselves?

1. DISCOVER ONE SONG OF YOUTH CULTURE THAT PROCLAIMS A POSITIVE VALUE. This might mean you will have to go to a music store to be able to read the lyrics. If you are a young person yourself, you may want to find some lyrics of a previous generation that really speak to you. Another alternative for adults would be to find a positive value in a youth-oriented movie. Utilize what you learn of this song or movie when witnessing to a person of the other culture.

2. FIND A DISTINCTIVE SUBCULTURE IN YOUR TOWN AND LEARN WHAT THIS SUBCULTURE VALUES. Talk to members of this subculture. Who are their "poets"? How do their values compare to what Scripture says?

3. DISCOVER HOW YOUR WORSHIP SERVICES CAN SPEAK TO THE YOUTH CULTURE. What will you need to do differently in your music?

CARING TIME
Remain in groups of 6–8 people, in a horseshoe configuration.

Hand out the Prayer/ Praise Report to the entire group. Ask each subgroup to pray for the empty chair. Pray specifically for God to guide you to someone to bring next week to fill that chair.

After a sufficient time of prayer in subgroups, close in a corporate prayer. Say, "Next week we will talk about: 'When Faith Is Bad for Business.' "

Remind participants of the daily Scripture readings and reflective questions found on page 107.

Caring Time (15-20 minutes)

During this time, have everyone in the group share prayer requests and pray for one another. Begin by having each member answer the question:

"If you had Paul before you right now,
what would be the biggest question in relation to God
that you would want him to address?"

Pray for guidance on these questions. In addition, pray for the concerns on the Prayer/Praise Report.

notes:

BIBLE STUDY NOTES

Reference Notes

Use these notes to gain further understanding of the text as you study on your own:

ACTS 17:17

Paul preached not only in the synagogue at Athens, but also in their marketplace where, three centuries before, Socrates likewise debated with anyone who would listen.

ACTS 17:18
philosophy

Epicurean and Stoic philosophers. Epicurus maintained that a tranquil life free from pain, passions, and fears was the highest good for humanity. This could be achieved only by detaching oneself from indulgence and the cares of the world. The Epicureans were practical atheists in that they believed the gods had no interest in humanity and were unknowable. The Stoics had a pantheistic idea of god as the World-Soul. People were a spark of the divine; upon death one's immortal soul would be absorbed into the divine spirit. The ideal life was one of virtue that refused to give in before the pressures of circumstances and of human passions.

this babbler. Literally, "seed-picker." A derisive term stemming from the actions of a bird that picks up seeds wherever it can find them. To the philosophers, Paul seemed like someone who picked up scraps of ideas here and there and then had the audacity to try to teach others.

foreign gods ... Jesus and the resurrection. Since the Greek word for

ACTS 17:18
philosophy
(cont'd)

Jesus sounds something like the Greek name for the goddess of health, and since the Greek word for salvation is also used to speak of physical healing, his listeners thought Paul was talking about two new gods—Health and Resurrection.

ACTS 17:19
credibility

Areopagus. Athens was a free city within the Roman Empire so the Areopagus had legal and judicial authority over what went on in the city. It does not appear that Paul himself is on trial (as though he was accused of breaking any laws) as much as his message itself is being evaluated as to its credibility and worth.

ACTS 17:21
deceived

Luke's rather sarcastic observation about the nature of the Athenian in general is an echo of what the Greek orator Demosthenes had said 400 years earlier: "You are the best people at being deceived by something new that is said."

ACTS 17:23

TO AN UNKNOWN GOD. Other writers of the time speak of statues and altars in Athens raised to gods "both known and unknown." The implicit admission of ignorance about God provided Paul with a point of entry for sharing the gospel.

ACTS 17:24

Paul asserts that God is not the uninterested or distant god of Greek philosophy.

does not live in temples. Euripides, a Greek philosopher, recognized this when he wrote, "What house built by craftsman could enclose the ... divine within enfolding walls?"

ACTS 17:25

he is not served by human hands. With this, the philosopher would also agree. Plato had written, "What advantage accrues to the gods from what they get from us?"

ACTS 17:26
God's creation

The Athenians had a tradition that they were different from other people in that they had sprung up from the soil of Athens itself (they were unique among other Greeks in that they had no tradition of how their ancestors migrated into the area). Paul's point is that they, like all people, derive from God's creation of humanity.

ACTS 17:27
knowing God

Challenging the Epicurean assumption that God was unknowable, Paul says that God is knowable by those who seek after Him. While the Stoics would agree with the nearness of God, the ideas of His separateness from creation and that one could know God personally would challenge them.

ACTS 17:28
truth revealed

Paul supports his points by quoting two Greek authors, Epimenides and Aratus. Both are from works about Zeus, and both were interpreted by the Stoics to refer to the *Logos*, the supreme source of reason and pride in the universe. These quotes do not imply Paul is equating Zeus with God, but it does indicate he recognized that God revealed truth about Himself even through other religions and philosophies.

ACTS 17:30

God overlooked such ignorance. This reflects the Old Testament notion that sins committed in ignorance are less culpable than those done in defiance.

ACTS 17:32–34
conversion

The converts included Dionysius, a member of the Athenian council. Nothing more is said in the New Testament about Athens, so it is unlikely that these believers established a church at the time.

[1] Rick Warren, *The Purpose-Driven Church* (Grand Rapids, MI: Zondervan Publishing House, 1995), p. 55.

Session 12

When Faith is "Bad for Business"

Prepare for the Session

	READINGS	REFLECTIVE QUESTIONS
Monday	Acts 19:23-27	How have your business dealings reflected your beliefs? Is there anything that needs to change?
Tuesday	Acts 19:28-34	In what difficult situation do you need to stand up for Christ? What obstacles are in your way?
Wednesday	Acts 19:35-41	Does anyone have a grievance against you? How can you reconcile with this person?
Thursday	Acts 23:6-11	What are you needing courage to do at this moment in your life? Can you trust God to give you this courage?
Friday	Acts 24:10-16	Is your conscience clear? If not, what do you need to do to make it clear? Make a confession? Appeal to God's grace?
Saturday	Acts 26:22-29	Are you trying to free people of their "chains" or put them in the same "chains" that shackle you?
Sunday	Acts 27:27-29	What is anchoring your life right now? Are your "anchors" holding when you go through "storms"?

notes:

OUR GOALS FOR THIS SESSION ARE:

In groups of 6–8, gather people in a horseshoe configuration.

Make sure everyone has a name tag.

Take time to share information on class parties that are coming up as well as any relevant church events.

INTRODUCE THE ICEBREAKER ACTIVITY: The students have been told in their books to choose one answer.

After the Icebreaker, say something like, "Some of us have doubtlessly caused more 'riots' than others. But Paul was one who always seemed to be at the center of a riot. Why was that so? In today's session, we will look at one such incident and see what we can find out."

Hand out the Prayer/Praise Report. A sample copy is on pages 158-159. Have people write down prayer requests and praises. Then have the prayer coordinator collect the report and make copies for use during the Caring Time.

BIBLE STUDY

- to consider how the gospel affected business interests in Ephesus
- to consider the relationship of faith to business practices
- to appreciate what it means to make Christ Lord of all of our life

LIFE CHANGE

- to gather a support group of other Christians in a similar line of work to help each other deal with ethical dilemmas
- to affirm one person in authority above us, in his sensitivity to the need for ethical business practices
- to pray daily for our business and ask for God's guidance on how to work ethically and effectively at the same time

Icebreaker (10-15 minutes)

What a Riot! Go around the group on question 1 and have everyone answer. Then go around again on question 2.

1. Which of the following situations would most likely raise a riot in your household? (For those living alone, which would have raised a riot in your family of origin?)

   - ☐ the television goes on the fritz
   - ☐ the mother takes a full-time job
   - ☐ one of the kids is asked to do a job they don't normally do
   - ☐ dinner isn't ready on time
   - ☐ the men have to iron their own clothes
   - ☐ the telephone is out of order
   - ☐ one bathroom is out of order and the other held hostage by a teenager
   - ☐ a parent tries to clean up a teenager's room

notes:

12

Icebreaker (cont'd)

2. Finish this sentence: "The way I personally would be most likely to cause a riot would be by ..."
   - ☐ stereotyping women while at a NOW convention.
   - ☐ wearing my swimsuit in public.
   - ☐ rooting for the other team while at the home team's park.
   - ☐ being loud and obnoxious at a demonstration for my favorite cause.
   - ☐ going too slow in the fast lane.
   - ☐ making a scene at a nice restaurant over food that wasn't what I ordered.
   - ☐ other: ______________________________

notes:

LEARNING FROM THE BIBLE

ACTS 19:23-41

Have three members of the class, selected ahead of time, read the passage from Acts. One member should read the narrative portion. The second should read the part of Demetrius (vv. 25b-27); and the third the part of the city clerk (vv. 35b-40). The whole class should read the part of the crowd (vv. 28b, 34b).

Bible Study (30-45 minutes)

The Scripture for this week:

23 About that time there arose a great disturbance about the Way.
24 A silversmith named Demetrius, who made silver shrines of Artemis,
brought in no little business for the craftsmen. 25 He called them
together, along with the workmen in related trades, and said: "Men,
you know we receive a good income from this business. 26 And you see
and hear how this fellow Paul has convinced and led astray large
numbers of people here in Ephesus and in practically the whole
province of Asia. He says that man-made gods are no gods at all.
27 There is danger not only that our trade will lose its good name, but
also that the temple of the great goddess Artemis will be discredited,
and the goddess herself, who is worshiped throughout the province of
Asia and the world, will be robbed of her divine majesty."

[28]When they heard this, they were furious and began shouting: "Great is Artemis of the Ephesians!" [29]Soon the whole city was in an uproar. The people seized Gaius and Aristarchus, Paul's traveling companions from Macedonia, and rushed as one man into the theater. [30]Paul wanted to appear before the crowd, but the disciples would not let him. [31]Even some of the officials of the province, friends of Paul, sent him a message begging him not to venture into the theater.

[32]The assembly was in confusion: Some were shouting one thing, some another. Most of the people did not even know why they were there. [33]The Jews pushed Alexander to the front, and some of the crowd shouted instructions to him. He motioned for silence in order to make a defense before the people. [34]But when they realized he was a Jew, they all shouted in unison for about two hours: "Great is Artemis of the Ephesians!"

[35]The city clerk quieted the crowd and said: "Men of Ephesus, doesn't all the world know that the city of Ephesus is the guardian of the temple of the great Artemis and of her image, which fell from heaven? [36]Therefore, since these facts are undeniable, you ought to be quiet and not do anything rash. [37]You have brought these men here, though they have neither robbed temples nor blasphemed our goddess. [38]If, then, Demetrius and his fellow craftsmen have a grievance against anybody, the courts are open and there are proconsuls. They can press charges. [39]If there is anything further you want to bring up, it must be settled in a legal assembly. [40]As it is, we are in danger of being charged with rioting because of today's events. In that case we would not be able to account for this commotion, since there is no reason for it." [41]After he had said this, he dismissed the assembly.

notes:

Summarize these introductory remarks. Be sure to include the underlined information, which gives the answers to the student book questions (provided in the margin).

What securities trader was known for his assertion "greed is good"? What happened to him?

What three things took ethics prisoner-of-war in the 1990s?

...about today's session (5 minutes)

MAINTAINING INTEGRITY

We live in a society where far too many people question whether business and ethical behavior can ever be compatible. Perhaps that is because of the high profile given in the past to such business people as former securities trader Ivan Boesky, who once said, "Greed is all right, by the way. I want you to know that. I think greed is healthy." Boesky was later involved in a serious fraud that further eroded America's faith in the ethics of business and sent him to jail.[1] William D. Lawrence of the Center for Christian Leadership at Dallas Theological Seminary, has written, "In the 1990s ethics appears to be missing in action, taken prisoner-of-war by greed, ambition, and selfish individualism. ... nowhere is the sickness more apparent than in corporate America and the financial community."[2] Now into the twenty-first century, there is little evidence things have improved.

In the midst of this ethical crisis, the Bible challenges us and our business leaders to realize that there is something more important than business profit. Maintaining integrity and holding to the Lordship of Jesus Christ must have priority for us over any business interest.

The conflict between business interest and Christian faith, however, is not new to the present day. We can find it in the Bible as well. As we look at our story this week, we find a situation where the gospel preached by Paul conflicted with the business interests of the city of Ephesus. The resulting outcry would rival any we might hear in our own time. As we study this story, perhaps we can come to some understanding of how to keep Christ as Lord and Master over our business interests today.

notes:

Remain in groups of 6–8 people, in a horseshoe configuration.

In this small-group session, students will be responding to the following questions that will help them share their stories in terms of the riot in Ephesus.

Have the students explore these questions together.

Identifying with the Story (5-7 minutes)

1. In this story, I identify most with:
   - ☐ Demetrius—because I have to deal with do-gooders who hurt my business.
   - ☐ the craftsmen—because I'm easily aroused to anger.
   - ☐ Gaius and Aristarchus—generally I'm the "innocent bystander" who gets dragged in.
   - ☐ the friendly officials of the province—I always have to get someone out of hot water.
   - ☐ the city clerk—I'm generally one who does things by orderly process.
   - ☐ Paul—I cause a lot of trouble just telling it like it is.
2. When have you been in a place where, like some in this crowd, you didn't even know why you were there?
   - ☐ in a church worship service
   - ☐ at a family reunion or gathering
   - ☐ in a church business or committee meeting
   - ☐ at work
   - ☐ at a party or social function
   - ☐ when I went to college
   - ☐ This describes most of my life!
   - ☐ other: ____________________
3. In moments of crisis, who has supplied the "voice of reason" in your life, like the city clerk supplied in Ephesus?
   - ☐ one of my parents
   - ☐ my spouse
   - ☐ myself
   - ☐ a friend
   - ☐ nobody—and I need that!
   - ☐ nobody—and I'm glad—I hate it when people are so reasonable!

notes:

12

today's session (15-20 minutes)

Share with your class the following information which you may modify according to your own perspectives and teaching needs. The answers to the student book questions (provided in the margin) are underlined.

In our last session, we looked at the need to speak in the language of our various subcultures about the truth of the gospel. But we must also remember that sometimes the truth of the gospel means *challenging* whatever culture to which we are speaking. One of the aspects of our culture we especially need to challenge is our money-first orientation. Right now, we have a culture that emphasizes money over people. When college students today are interviewed about their goals in life, the number one response that comes up is "to make a lot of money." This emphasis shows up in the popular culture in various forms. Madonna's theme song became "Material Girl," in which she declared that any guy who wanted to have a chance with her needed to have money. Even back in the more idealistic era of the 60s and 70s, the Beatles sang, "They say the best things in life are free, but you can tell that to the birds and bees—give me money, that's what I want!" In the movie *Jerry Maguire*, a central character repeated the saying, "Show me the money!" and it became a statement on the mouths of many in our culture. Unfortunately, this approach is not peculiar to our time and culture, as we see in our Scripture passage.

What saying from the movie* Jerry Maguire *typifies our culture's obsession with money?

Paul's Mission in Ephesus

Paul had one of his most successful mission ventures in Ephesus. He worked there for approximately three years. Paul's typical pattern of being driven out of town by the Jewish religious leadership—never happened here. Instead, opposition eventually came from a far more mundane direction. A silversmith named Demetrius aroused his fellow craftsmen into a frenzy because Paul was getting people to turn away from their handcrafted goddesses. Essentially, the people of Ephesus were saying, "It's all right to teach whatever you want—just don't let it interfere with business!" In this city the silver trade had become big because there were gods and goddesses to be made. The silversmith trade especially made a great deal of money through the manufacture and sale of models of the goddess Artemis. Artemis was a goddess who combined belief in the Roman virgin goddess Diana with an Asian fertility goddess. The center for her worship was in Ephesus where an image of her (actually a meteorite) was placed in a temple that was one of the seven wonders of the ancient world. In the spring, there was a festival in her honor marked by crowds flocking to Ephesus for a celebration that included orgies and general carousing. Teaching that there was one God, who was not made with human hands, and that He demanded right living and sexual responsibility really interfered with this business-building festival!

How long did Paul's mission in Ephesus last?

What goddess was at the center of the silversmith trade in Ephesus?

When People Stop Listening

What did the craftsmen of Ephesus do to avoid listening to any voice of reason?

Once Demetrius had convinced the craftsmen that their livelihood was at stake, they stopped listening to anyone else. They repeatedly yelled out, "Great is Artemis of the Ephesians!" (v. 28). Alexander was almost able to quiet them down to listen, until they realized that he was a Jew. The people of Ephesus didn't make any distinction between Jew and Christian at this time. As far as they were concerned, they were all part of that Jewish faith that insisted on worshiping one God, and didn't tolerate gods made by their hands. So then we are told they went on shouting "Great is Artemis of the Ephesians" for two more hours!

It's hard to listen when your income is threatened. Those who have been involved in strikes or lockouts know that. But what many also know is that when people stop listening, nothing is solved. Truth or logic no longer hold weight—it is all emotion.

What problems arise when we make money our security?

People become emotional over their income because it is their security. And when money is our security we make everything else—from morality to the people in our life—take a backseat. The people we work with are stepping stones to get to the top. Customers become account numbers, and our goal becomes not serving people through providing needed products, but whatever will enhance the bottom line. Even our families come in second to money sometimes. When it comes to choosing between closing the deal and being there for a family member at an important event, too often we choose the deal. Ironically, the money that we thought of as our security can end up destroying a secure family life.

True Security

What did Jesus say we should seek first?

True security comes from making Jesus Christ Lord of our life—including business. That is what Jesus himself meant when he said, "But seek first his kingdom and his righteousness, and all these things [food, clothing, shelter] will be given to you as well" (Matt. 6:33). Making Christ Lord of your life means seeking from Him the direction that helps you keep your personal life, your business life, and your spiritual life all in a proper balance. When we are faced with a tough ethical decision, we need to take it to Him. When we are looking for a way to do the right thing, and yet take care of our business responsibilities, we need to take it to Him. When our family calls us home at the same time business calls us to the office, we need to take it to Him. If we make these decisions by our own wisdom and insight alone, we risk making a shambles of our life. When we seek God's help and direction, we have a better chance of keeping our lives together.

today's session (cont'd)

The Ephesian silversmiths shut their ears to everything in their emotional clinging to "business as usual." But they were clinging to an empty way of life. The days of their craft were numbered, and they were living under the illusion that something they made with their own hands could be a god. Will we make the same mistake?

notes:

Remain in groups of 6–8 people, in a horseshoe configuration.

In this small-group session, students will be applying the lessons of the text to their own lives through the following questions.

The students were asked (in the student book) to choose an answer for each question and explain why.

Learning from the Story (5-7 minutes)

1. Had you been called upon to moderate the dispute between Paul and the "local silversmith's union," what might you have said?

2. If you were to put a percentage on the degree Demetrius was concerned with his income, and the degree he was concerned about Artemis being robbed of her "divine majesty," what percentage would you assign to both?
   - ☐ 10% income; 90% "divine majesty"
   - ☐ 25% income; 75% "divine majesty"
   - ☐ 50% income; 50% "divine majesty"
   - ☐ 75% income; 25% "divine majesty"
   - ☐ 90% income; 10% "divine majesty"

3. How would you finish this sentence: "When Christian faith implies things that seem bad for business, a Christian should ..."

Share with the class the following thoughts on how the lessons of this text might be applied today. The answers to the student book questions (provided in the margin) are underlined unless the question requires a personal answer.

What electronics firm is pointed to as an example of a successful, ethical business?

What biblical characters remind us of how God provides for those who confront powerful forces and stand their ground?

life change lessons (5-7 minutes)

For many people, one of the hardest areas of life in which to put Christ's teaching into practice is their business or professional life. Some feel that if they truly acted in an ethical manner, they would lose their job or their business would go bankrupt. Jack Turpin, founder of <u>Hall-Mark Electronics</u>, which eventually became the third largest electronics distributor in the United States, believes differently. William D. Lawrence writes of this venture, "Though making a profit and holding its own against competitors certainly are corporate goals, the strategy by which Hall-Mark achieved these goals makes it distinctive. Beyond the bottom line, where a person's faith and his business practices meet, Jack Turpin has conducted the business with spiritual choices and ethical standards clearly in view."[3] People who conduct business according to Christian ethical standards inspire consumer trust, and that brings business.

For a person who works for someone else the process may be harder. Sometimes it means having to convince management that ethical practices make practical sense. If that fails, then standing up for ethical practices can endanger your job. <u>But then we should remember biblical characters like Moses</u>, <u>Joseph</u>, <u>or Daniel</u>, <u>who stood with God against powerful forces and were rewarded in the end for their faithfulness</u>.

On a practical level, defending ethical business practices can start with these specific changes:

1. GATHER A SUPPORT GROUP OF OTHER CHRISTIANS IN A SIMILAR LINE OF WORK TO HELP EACH OTHER DEAL WITH ETHICAL DILEMMAS. This could be other Christians where you work, or other Christian business people. Those not in your business may not understand the pressures you are under, but they probably have similar situations of their own.

2. AFFIRM ONE PERSON IN AUTHORITY ABOVE YOU IN HIS SENSITIVITY TO THE NEED FOR ETHICAL BUSINESS PRACTICES. Start by observing those you work with. Make an effort to look for positive signs and comment when an honest concern for Christian ethics is exhibited.

3. PRAY DAILY FOR YOUR BUSINESS AND ASK FOR GOD'S GUIDANCE ON HOW TO WORK ETHICALLY AND EFFECTIVELY AT THE SAME TIME. James assures us that, "The prayer of the righteous is powerful and effective" (Jas. 5:16b, NRSV). Here is an important way to claim that promise. Make sure that you include prayer for the leaders of your business as well as the issues that you face together.

CARING TIME
Remain in groups of 6–8 people, in a horseshoe configuration.

Hand out the Prayer/ Praise Report to the entire group. Ask each subgroup to pray for the empty chair. Pray specifically for God to guide you to someone to bring next week to fill that chair.

After a sufficient time of prayer in subgroups, close in a corporate prayer. Say, "Next week we will talk about: 'An Irrepressible Boldness.' "

Remind participants of the daily Scripture readings and reflective questions found on page 117.

Caring Time (15-20 minutes)

Come together now for a time of sharing and prayer. Begin by having each person in the group finish the statement:

"The area of my life that seems really chaotic right now is ..."

Pray for these areas of concern, and for the concerns listed on the Prayer/Praise Report.

notes:

BIBLE STUDY NOTES

Reference Notes

Use these notes to gain further understanding of the text as you study on your own:

ACTS 19:24
idol worship

A silversmith. The silversmith trade made a great deal of money through the manufacture and sale of models of the goddess Artemis. Artemis was a goddess who combined belief in the Roman virgin goddess Diana with an Asian fertility goddess. The center for her worship was in Ephesus where an image of her (actually a meteorite) was placed in a temple that was one of the seven wonders of the ancient world. In the spring, there was a festival in her honor marked by crowds flocking to Ephesus for a celebration that included orgies and general carousing.

ACTS 19:29
accusation

Gaius and Aristarchus. These men were among those who accompanied Paul when he left Ephesus (20:4). Unable to find Paul, the crowd grabbed two of his associates to accuse.
The theater. While this was the usual place for public meetings, it would have been especially appropriate in this case since the great temple of Artemis could be clearly seen from it.

ACTS 19:30–31
protection

Both the Christians and some of the officials (these were the *asiarchs*, the chief citizens out of whose ranks the officials of the Roman cult of emperor worship were elected for one-year terms of office) urged Paul not to go into the theater for fear of his safety. The protection of the *asiarchs* is another example of official Roman protection and tolerance of Paul (18:14-17).

ACTS 19:33–34
against idolatry

The Jews, perhaps to disassociate themselves from the charges being made against Paul, tried to have one of their number (Alexander) make a statement. However, since the Jews were well known to be against idolatry as well, he was shouted down by the crowd before he could even speak.

ACTS 19:35
peacemaker

The city clerk. This was the highest-ranking official in the city, accountable to the Roman provincial government for what happened in Ephesus. Not wanting to be charged with rioting, which could lead to penalties for the city, he worked to quiet down the crowd and dismiss them.
her image, which fell from heaven. See note above on 19:24.

ACTS 19:37

robbed temples. Wealthy people would deposit treasures at temples for safekeeping in light of the sacred nature of the place.

ACTS 19:38

proconsuls. Provinces that did not require troops to maintain order were administered by the Roman Senate through a proconsul. Typically, there was only one at a time over a given area.

ACTS 19:39

legal assembly. The people could gather for meetings to discuss issues that concerned them, but they were to be held at set times and with a set procedure. Such an irregular, chaotic meeting as this one could lead to Roman suppression of their right to assemble. The crowd, mindful of the implied warning, dispersed.

notes:

[1] Quoted in William D. Lawrence, "Beyond the Bottom Line: Where Faith and Business Meet," (Chicago: Moody Press, 1994), p. 25.
[2] Ibid., pp. 13,16.
[3] Ibid., pp. 43–44.

Session 13

An Irrepressible Boldness

Prepare for the Session

	READINGS	REFLECTIVE QUESTIONS
Monday	Acts 28:1-6	From what "vipers" has God protected you? Have you given Him the glory for this?
Tuesday	Acts 28:15-16	Who has gone out of their way for you? Have you thanked God for them?
Wednesday	Acts 28:17-20	How has your hope in Christ taken you through trials? Has that hope remained strong?
Thursday	Acts 28:21-23	How persistent are you in sharing your faith in Christ?
Friday	Acts 28:24-26	What have you heard from teachers of the faith that you still don't understand? Who could help you to a clearer understanding?
Saturday	Acts 28:27-28	To what has your heart become calloused? People in need? The call of God? Pray for God to touch your heart anew.
Sunday	Acts 28:30-31	What would it mean for you to "boldly and without hindrance" live out your faith in Christ?

notes:

OUR GOALS FOR THIS SESSION ARE:

In groups of 6–8, gather people in a horseshoe configuration.

Make sure everyone has a name tag.

Take time to share information on class parties that are coming up as well as any relevant church events.

INTRODUCE THE ICEBREAKER ACTIVITY: The students have been told in their books to choose one answer.

After the Icebreaker, say something like, "While these warrants are meant to be less than serious, the arrest of Paul at the end of Acts was a grave matter. Some scholars believe that he was executed at the end of this imprisonment. Still, Paul used this experience for God's glory. In today's session, we will see how he did so."

Hand out the Prayer/Praise Report. A sample copy is on pages 158-159. Have people write down prayer requests and praises. Then have the prayer coordinator collect the report and make copies for use during the Caring Time.

BIBLE STUDY
- to see how Paul's boldness in witnessing was not suppressed by his imprisonment
- to consider what it means to boldly witness for Christ today
- to encourage Christians to witness, even when in tough circumstances

LIFE CHANGE
- to write out a brief statement of what Christ has done for us
- to make a list of those to whom God is leading us
- to share our story with the people on our list, after praying for them

Icebreaker (10-15 minutes)

Group Warrants. Normally groups try to build an atmosphere of supportiveness, but this time we are asking you to turn "state's evidence" against your other group members! Decide which of your group members ought to be served with each of the following warrants. Write the name of one group member next to each category. Then go around the group, one person at a time, and have the others serve their warrants.

__________ for Grand Theft—You stole our hearts with your warmth.

__________ for Assault—You fought against the pretenses we try to use to hide the truth from ourselves and others.

__________ for Insurrection—You stood up against the values of this world.

__________ for Reckless Driving—You steered us through some dangerous areas with little thought of playing it safe.

__________ for Aiding and Abetting—You nurtured the spiritual growth of the group.

__________ for Creating a Disturbance—Your humor and crazy ways kept things from getting too predictable.

__________ for Arson—You set the group on fire with the Spirit.

notes:

LEARNING FROM THE BIBLE

ACTS 28:16-31

Have one member of the class, selected ahead of time, read the passage from Acts.

Bible Study (30-45 minutes)

The Scripture for this week:

[16]When we got to Rome, Paul was allowed to live by himself,
with a soldier to guard him.
[17]Three days later he called together the leaders of the Jews.
When they had assembled, Paul said to them: "My brothers, although
I have done nothing against our people or against the customs of our
ancestors, I was arrested in Jerusalem and handed over to the
Romans. [18]They examined me and wanted to release me, because I
was not guilty of any crime deserving death. [19]But when the Jews
objected, I was compelled to appeal to Caesar—not that I had any
charge to bring against my own people. [20]For this reason I have asked
to see you and talk with you. It is because of the hope of Israel that
I am bound with this chain."
[21]They replied, "We have not received any letters from Judea con-
cerning you, and none of the brothers who have come from there has
reported or said anything bad about you. [22]But we want to hear what
your views are, for we know that people everywhere are talking
against this sect."
[23]They arranged to meet Paul on a certain day, and came in even
larger numbers to the place where he was staying. From morning till
evening he explained and declared to them the kingdom of God and
tried to convince them about Jesus from the Law of Moses and from
the Prophets. [24]Some were convinced by what he said, but others
would not believe. [25]They disagreed among themselves and began to
leave after Paul had made this final statement: "The Holy Spirit spoke
the truth to your forefathers when he said through Isaiah the prophet:

[26]" 'Go to this people and say,
"You will be ever hearing but never understanding;
you will be ever seeing but never perceiving."
[27]For this people's heart has become calloused;
they hardly hear with their ears,
and they have closed their eyes.
Otherwise they might see with their eyes,
hear with their ears,
understand with their hearts
and turn, and I would heal them.'

[28]"Therefore I want you to know that God's salvation has been
sent to the Gentiles, and they will listen!"

30For two whole years Paul stayed there in his own rented house and welcomed all who came to see him. 31Boldly and without hindrance he preached the kingdom of God and taught about the Lord Jesus Christ.

notes:

Summarize these introductory remarks. Be sure to include the underlined information, which gives the answers to the student book questions (provided in the margin).

What were some of the things that happened in the life of Paul between last week's study and this week's?

Why was Paul brought to Rome?

...about today's session (5 minutes)

BOLDNESS IN OUR MISSION

Over the past weeks, we have been looking at what made the church of the first century so vital. We have considered things like their fellowship, their prayer life, their multicultural makeup, and their connection to the Holy Spirit. All of these things came together to produce a church that believed in its mission to share the gospel with the whole world. That resulted in boldness. The Apostle Paul typified that boldness. There is a gap between the text we will look at today and what we looked at last week. Paul had been to Jerusalem to deliver an offering he had collected from his churches for the poor people of Jerusalem. But while there his opponents accused him of violating the temple by bringing a Gentile into it, a crime that would have been punishable by death (Acts 21:17-36). After a long process of argument and trial, Paul appealed to be judged by Caesar and so was delivered to Rome, which is where this session begins. In all of these tensions and negotiations, Paul never lost his boldness in proclaiming that Jesus Christ is the Savior of the world.

The modern church has sometimes lost its boldness, however. And so as we study this passage today, let us concentrate on what we can learn to revitalize our sense of mission.

Remain in groups of 6–8 people, in a horseshoe configuration.

In this small-group session, students will be responding to the following questions that will help them share their stories in terms of Paul's bold witness in Rome.

Have the students explore these questions together.

Identifying with the Story (5-7 minutes)

1. Finish this sentence in one of the following ways, or pick your own: "The most trouble I have been in with the law was when ..."
   - ☐ I went joyriding as an adolescent.
   - ☐ I shoplifted as a child or adolescent.
   - ☐ well, there was that traffic ticket ...
   - ☐ my taxes were audited.
   - ☐ I tore off that mattress tag that says, "Do not remove under penalty of law."
   - ☐ "I would tell you ... but then I would have to kill you!"
   - ☐ other: ______________________

2. For whom in your life does it seem true that when you speak, they "hardly hear with their ears" (v. 27)?
   - ☐ my children
   - ☐ my parents
   - ☐ the government
   - ☐ my spouse
   - ☐ my boss
   - ☐ other: ____________

3. If you were called before a group of people to defend how you have lived your life, as Paul was, what would you say?

notes:

today's session (15-20 minutes)

Share with your class the following information which you may modify according to your own perspectives and teaching needs. The answers to the student book questions (provided in the margin) are underlined.

In Acts 4:13, why was the Sanhedrin amazed at the boldness of Peter and John?

In the Book of Acts there is a consistent connection between the presence of the Holy Spirit and the boldness with which the disciples acted. The words "boldly" and "boldness" or their equivalent are used eight different times: Acts 4:13,29,31; 9:27-28; 13:46; 14:3; 18:26; 19:8. To understand our passage it might be best to first look at 4:13. It says there, "Now when they [the Sanhedrin, a kind of Jewish Supreme Court] saw the boldness of Peter and John and realized that they were uneducated and ordinary men, they were amazed and recognized them as companions of Jesus" (NRSV). What is the connection between the first phrase of this sentence and the second? Boldness and (probably) eloquence did not go together in the minds of these educated religious leaders with "uneducated and ordinary men." This started them thinking, "In what other person have we seen this behavior?" Immediately they thought of Jesus the prophet from Nazareth. Boldness was a mark of having been with Christ. When you think about it, that is a natural reaction. When you realize that even death can't defeat you, isn't it natural to be bold?

Paul's Arrival in Rome

What were some of the letters Paul probably wrote while imprisoned in Rome?

The passage we just looked at is near the beginning of the Book of Acts. But now let's look at our main passage for this week, which is at the end of the Book of Acts. Paul had been arrested in Jerusalem and transferred to prison in Rome. In verse 16 we learn of the conditions under which he lived. At first he was given a fair amount of freedom. Basically, he was under house arrest. This freedom is what allowed him to write the letters he wrote while a prisoner in Rome. These include Ephesians (Eph. 4:1; 6:19-20); Philippians (Phil. 1:7,12-14,19-26); Colossians (Col. 4:3-4,18); and Philemon (Philem. 1,9,13). Philippians 1:12-13 gives an insight to his situation during this time as he carried on an extensive ministry to the soldiers assigned to guard him, undoubtedly resulting in the conversion of a number of them.

What are two perspectives on the end result of Paul's imprisonment at Rome?

Verses 17-22 tell a few minimal facts about his attempts to defend himself while in Rome. What was the end result of all of this? While some believe that at the end of these two years Paul was executed, other scholars contend that Paul was released and enjoyed freedom for another two years, during which he traveled once again to Crete, Asia, and Macedonia. It was during this time that it is believed he wrote the letters of 1 Timothy and Titus. According to this second perspective, he was again arrested and imprisoned at Rome, but this time things were far more sinister. The Emperor Nero, widely suspected of having started the great fire of Rome in A.D. 64, needed to shift the blame off of himself onto someone else, and Christians were chosen as the culprits. This resulted in an outburst of cruel persecution against the church during which it is believed both Paul (by being beheaded) and Peter (by being crucified upside down) were executed by Roman authorities.

In the last verses in Acts (vv. 30-31), the emphasis in the Greek sentence falls on the boldness and freedom with which Paul preached the gospel. Luke concludes Acts with the picture of Paul continuing his missionary activities and preaching to all who would listen. He may have been able to work as a tentmaker and leather-worker during this time. Also, gifts from the churches that cared for him may have provided for his needs (Phil. 4:14-18).

The Meaning of Boldness

What did proclaiming Christ with boldness mean for Paul?

Proclaiming Christ with boldness meant several things for Paul. It meant proclaiming Christ without shame or apology. This is what Christ called for in Luke 9:26, when he said, "If anyone is ashamed of me and my words, the Son of Man will be ashamed of him when he comes in his glory and in the glory of the Father and of the holy angels." An example of Paul proclaiming Christ in this spirit can be found in 1 Corinthians 1:18-25, where he proclaims the Cross, even though some treat it as foolishness.

Boldness meant for Paul to proclaim Christ without compromising with the world's standards. Again, he wrote in 1 Corinthians 2:6, "We do, however, speak a message of wisdom among the mature, but not the wisdom of this age or of the rulers of this age, who are coming to nothing."

Boldness meant proclaiming Christ with passion and conviction. Proclaiming Christ with passion and conviction does not mean without tact or consideration of others, like some do in their street corner harangues. Nor does it mean being bullheaded and refusing to listen. But it does mean to proclaim Christ with full confidence that God is speaking through us and will make the message fruitful. That is the boldness that God gave to Paul.

Why had friends warned Paul not to go to Jerusalem? Why did he go anyway?

Finally, boldness meant proclaiming Christ without fear. Before Paul went to Jerusalem, where he was eventually arrested and sent to Rome, his friends and supporters had warned him against going there (Acts 21:10-14). But no threat could keep Paul from his task. He said in Acts 20:22-24, "And now, compelled by the Spirit, I am going to Jerusalem, not knowing what will happen to me there. I only know that in every city the Holy Spirit warns me that prison and hardships are facing me. However, I consider my life worth nothing to me, if only I may finish the race and complete the task the Lord

Jesus has given me—the task of testifying to the gospel of God's grace." Paul faced violence of all kinds, including flogging, shipwrecks, and assault (2 Cor. 11:25-27), but none of it kept him from boldly proclaiming the gospel.

But is all of this a testimony to Paul—a biblical hero with virtues we could never hope to replicate? To answer this question we need only point to the truth with which we started: It was the presence of the Holy Spirit that gave Paul this boldness, and that same Holy Spirit can give us the boldness to do what God asks. That is a truth we need to rely on as we continue the story of the church that was just beginning in the Book of Acts.

notes:

Remain in groups of 6–8 people, in a horseshoe configuration.

In this small-group session, students will be applying the lessons of the text to their own lives through the following questions.

The students were asked (in the student book) to choose an answer for each question and explain why.

Learning from the Story (5-7 minutes)

1. How would you describe Paul as you see him in this last story of Acts? (Check as many characteristics as apply.)

- ☐ defensive
- ☐ optimistic
- ☐ zealous
- ☐ frustrated
- ☐ stubborn
- ☐ confident
- ☐ bold
- ☐ bitter
- ☐ irrepressible
- ☐ weary
- ☐ other: ________________

2. What would you say seems to be Paul's main concern in this passage?

- ☐ justifying his life
- ☐ spreading the gospel
- ☐ gaining his freedom
- ☐ denouncing his enemies
- ☐ other: ________________________________

3. The most influential factor in Paul being able to preach the gospel boldly while under arrest was:

- ☐ Paul's irrepressible personality
- ☐ the power of the Holy Spirit
- ☐ his knowledge that God was with him
- ☐ the companionship of believers who supported him
- ☐ other: ________________________________

Share with the class the following thoughts on how the lessons of this text might be applied today. The answers to the student book questions (provided in the margin) are underlined unless the question requires a personal answer.

What is the reason presented by the leader that many people today don't share their faith? Do you agree with this analysis?

"Boldness does not have to mean being ___________."

life change lessons (5-7 minutes)

The things we fear in developed countries of the twenty-first century are for the most part different than what was feared by Christians of the first century. We are not likely to be put in prison or stoned for declaring our faith in Jesus Christ. While travel dangers do exist to a degree, shipwrecks and bandits alongside the road are not the danger they used to be. All we have to fear is social rejection. So one would think that without such barriers it would be easier to be bold in our proclamation of Jesus Christ as Savior and Lord. And yet it would seem most Christians keep their faith quiet. To a degree this is because we don't like to be equated with the over-zealous persons we see giving evangelistic harangues on downtown street corners or harassing hurried, unwilling passersby in other public venues. Most people don't want to be seen as a public nuisance. But to a degree our quietness about our faith is a result of a lack of the kind of boldness typified by Paul and others in the Book of Acts. Our fears may only be social, but we let them intimidate us into quietly blending in.

Boldness does not have to mean being obnoxious. It can simply mean sharing honestly and enthusiastically with friends what Christ has done for us. It must be personal and it must include listening to people as well as sharing with them. Here are some important specific things we can do:

1. WRITE OUT A BRIEF STATEMENT OF WHAT CHRIST HAS DONE FOR YOU. This should be personal, not a repeat of what you have heard other people say. Don't memorize it in order to present it as a "canned spiel," but do learn the essence of it. It should be only a couple of paragraphs, and it should include how your Christian faith helps you deal with life today, and not just what happened at your conversion.

2. MAKE A LIST OF THOSE TO WHOM GOD IS LEADING YOU. Sharing faith is done most effectively with those we already know, not strangers on the street. Learn what the needs of these people are. Pray for those needs, as well as for their receptivity to the gospel message.

3. SHARE YOUR STORY WITH THE PEOPLE ON YOUR LIST, AFTER PRAYING FOR THEM. Make sure you have prayed for them at least for a week. Start out by asking them if they ever think about spiritual concerns. Hear their perspectives before sharing yours. Don't feel you have to make a long speech. Oftentimes, the first time you share you are just planting a seed that you can nurture over time.

CARING TIME
Remain in groups of 6–8 people, in a horseshoe configuration.

Hand out the Prayer/Praise Report to the group. Be sure to allow enough time for the evaluation. If your group is going to continue, also allow time to discuss the covenant on page 124. Close with a corporate prayer.

Caring Time (15-20 minutes)

Pray for the concerns listed on the Prayer/Praise Report, then continue with the evaluation and covenant.

1. Take some time to evaluate the life of your group by using the statements below. Read the first sentence out loud and ask everyone to explain where they would put a dot between the two extremes. When you are finished, go back and give your group an overall grade in the categories of Group Building, Bible Study, and Mission.

GROUP BUILDING

On celebrating life and having fun together, we were more like a ...
wet blanket · hot tub

On becoming a caring community, we were more like a ...
prickly porcupine · cuddly teddy bear

BIBLE STUDY

On sharing our spiritual stories, we were more like a ...
shallow pond · spring-fed lake

On digging into Scripture, we were more like a ...
slow-moving snail · · · · · · · · · · · · · · · · · · · voracious anteater

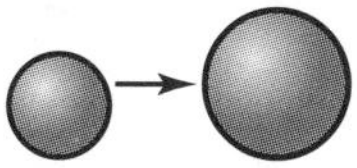

MISSION

On inviting new people into our group, we were more like a ...
barbed-wire fence · wide-open door

On stretching our vision for mission, we were more like an ...
ostrich · eagle

Caring Time (cont'd)

2. What are some specific areas in which you have grown in this course?

- ▢ being more open to the Holy Spirit's guidance
- ▢ finding new ways to minister to other's needs
- ▢ handling conflict situations in the church with love and wisdom
- ▢ sharing faith and fellowship with other cultures
- ▢ understanding the power of prayer
- ▢ slowing down and letting the Holy Spirit guide me
- ▢ following ethical business practices
- ▢ other:____________________________________

A covenant is a promise made to another in the presence of God. Its purpose is to indicate your intention to make yourselves available to one another for the fulfillment of the purposes you share in common. If your group is going to continue, in a spirit of prayer work your way through the following sentences, trying to reach an agreement on each statement pertaining to your ongoing life together. Write out your covenant like a contract, stating your purpose, goals, and the ground rules for your group.

1. The purpose of our group will be:

2. Our goals will be:

3. We will meet on ________________ (day of week).

4. We will meet for _____weeks, after which we will decide if we wish to continue as a group.

5. We will meet from _______ to _______ and we will strive to start on time and end on time.

6. We will meet at ____________________ (place) or we will rotate from house to house.

7. We will agree to the following ground rules for our group (check):

   - ▢ **PRIORITY:** While you are in this course of study, you give the group meetings priority.
   - ▢ **PARTICIPATION:** Everyone is encouraged to participate and no one dominates.
   - ▢ **RESPECT:** Everyone has the right to his or her own opinion, and all questions are encouraged and respected.
   - ▢ **CONFIDENTIALITY:** Anything said in the meeting is never repeated outside the meeting.
   - ▢ **LIFE CHANGE:** We will regularly assess our own life change goals and encourage one another in our pursuit of Christlikeness.
   - ▢ **EMPTY CHAIR:** The group stays open to reaching new people at every meeting.
   - ▢ **CARE and SUPPORT:** Permission is given to call upon each other at any time especially in times of crisis. The group will provide care for every member.
   - ▢ **ACCOUNTABILITY:** We agree to let the members of the group hold us accountable to the commitments which each of us make in whatever loving ways we decide upon.
   - ▢ **MISSION:** We will do everything in our power to start a new group.
   - ▢ **MINISTRY:** The group will encourage one another to volunteer and serve in a ministry, and to support missions by giving financially and/or personally serving.

notes:

BIBLE STUDY NOTES

Reference Notes

Use these notes to gain further understanding of the text as you study on your own:

ACTS 28:16
house arrest

Paul was allowed to live by himself. Paul was not kept in a prison, but kept under guard in a type of house arrest while he awaited trial. He may have been able to work as a leather-worker during this time, or gifts from the churches that cared for him may have provided for his needs (Phil. 4:14-18).

ACTS 28:17–22
first-hand account

As soon as possible, Paul called together the leaders of the synagogues in Rome (at least 13 are known to have existed). He held this meeting in order to explain his situation to them first-hand so they might not be influenced more by rumors than personal information.

ACTS 28:19
faithfulness

my own people. Notice also "my brothers" and "our ancestors" (v. 17). Once again, Luke presents Paul as a faithful Jew; his commitment to Jesus as the Messiah is to be seen as a natural outgrowth of his trust in the Old Testament Scriptures and his loyalty to God (v. 20; 23:6; 24:15; 26:22-23). His appeal to Caesar is not to be construed as trying to bring any problems to the Jews either in Rome or Jerusalem.

ACTS 28:22
seeking answers

people everywhere are talking about this sect. A church had been established among the Jewish community in Rome for at least 20 years and perhaps as far back as Pentecost nearly 30 years earlier (2:10). Paul's letter to Rome, written about three years before his arrival, deals extensively with conflicts arising between Jewish and Gentile elements in the church there. Thus, these Jewish leaders certainly knew something of Christianity, but they may have desired to finally get some answers to questions that had never been clearly explained to them.

ACTS 28:23
reign of God

Examples of how Paul argued for the gospel from the Old Testament Scriptures are given in 13:16-41; 22:3–21 and 26:4-27.

the kingdom of God. Throughout the Gospels, the message of Jesus is known as the message of the kingdom of God (Mark 1:15). This phrase serves as summary of what the entire gospel is about—it announces the present and coming reign of God in human affairs and calls people to affirm their loyalty to Jesus as God's appointed King.

ACTS 28:25–27
unbelief

Paul accounts for the unbelief of many through the words of the prophet Isaiah in Isaiah 6:9–10 (see also Mark 4:12). In its context, this passage spoke of the fact that although God sent Isaiah to call Israel to repent, the net effect of his preaching would be that people would become even more hardened against God. Verse 27 is full of a sad irony; it is as if the people deliberately block their ears and shut their eyes to God as though the last thing they want is to turn to God and be forgiven. By quoting this passage, Paul is calling on his Jewish hearers not to follow in the footsteps of their forefathers who rejected Isaiah and his message.

ACTS 28:30
holiness

Luke concludes Acts with the picture of Paul continuing his missionary activities and preaching to all who would listen.

his own rented house. See note on 28:16.

ACTS 28:31
boldly proclaiming the gospel

In this last statement in Acts, the emphasis in the Greek sentence falls on the boldness and freedom with which Paul preached the gospel. During this period of house arrest, Paul wrote the letter of Philippians and probably the letters of Ephesians, Colossians, and Philemon as well. Philippians 1:12-13 gives an insight to his situation during this time as he carried on an extensive ministry to the soldiers assigned to guard him, undoubtedly resulting in the conversion of a number of them. While some believe that at the end of these two years Paul was executed, other scholars contend that Paul was released and enjoyed freedom for another two years, during which he traveled once again to Crete, Asia, and Macedonia. It was during this time that it is believed he wrote the letters of 1 Timothy and Titus. According to this second perspective, at some point after this, he was again arrested and imprisoned at Rome, but this time things were far more sinister. The Emperor Nero, widely suspected of having started the great fire of Rome in A.D. 64, needed to shift the blame off of himself onto someone else and Christians were chosen as the culprits. This resulted in an outburst of cruel persecution against the church during which it is believed both Paul and Peter were executed by Roman authorities.

notes:

Pray / Praise Report

Name	Phone No.	Pray for ...	Praise God for ...